NATIVE PEOPLES
of North America

Daniel M. Cobb, Ph.D.

THE
GREAT
COURSES®

Smithsonian®

PUBLISHED BY:

THE GREAT COURSES
Corporate Headquarters
4840 Westfields Boulevard, Suite 500
Chantilly, Virginia 20151-2299
Phone: 1-800-832-2412
Fax: 703-378-3819
www.thegreatcourses.com

Copyright © The Teaching Company, 2016

Printed in the United States of America

This book is in copyright. All rights reserved.

Without limiting the rights under copyright reserved above,
no part of this publication may be reproduced, stored in
or introduced into a retrieval system, or transmitted,
in any form, or by any means
(electronic, mechanical, photocopying, recording, or otherwise),
without the prior written permission of
The Teaching Company.

Daniel M. Cobb, Ph.D.
Associate Professor of American Studies
The University of North Carolina at Chapel Hill

Daniel M. Cobb is an Associate Professor of American Studies at the University of North Carolina at Chapel Hill, where he has taught since 2010. He graduated cum laude with a B.A. in History and minor in Sociology from Messiah College. He received his M.A. and Ph.D. in History from the University of Wyoming and the University of Oklahoma, respectively. Dr. Cobb then served as assistant director of the Newberry Library's D'Arcy McNickle Center for American Indian and Indigenous Studies and as Assistant Professor of History at Miami University in Oxford, Ohio. At the University of North Carolina, he has been the director of undergraduate studies and the coordinator of the American Indian and Indigenous Studies major concentration and minor.

Dr. Cobb's research focuses on American Indian history since 1887, political activism, ethnohistorical methods, ethnobiography, memory, and global indigenous rights. He has extensive experience in public history and engaged scholarship, including serving as program director for a series of public events at Miami University devoted to American Indian politics and activism and as co-organizer for a seminar and public symposium on memory. Dr. Cobb created and installed an exhibit about the life and legacy of Ponca activist Clyde Warrior for the Ponca Tribe of Oklahoma's Clyde Warrior Memorial Building. He has for many years been involved in Teaching American History and other professional development programs for public school teachers. Dr. Cobb also has served as a consultant on public history for a consortium of the nation's leading museums, including the National Museum of the American Indian.

At Miami University, undergraduate students nominated Dr. Cobb as the Associated Student Government's Outstanding Professor of the Year for four consecutive years, and he was a nominee for the E. Phillips Knox Distinguished Teaching Award from the Center for Teaching Excellence for two consecutive years. At the University of North Carolina, he received the Tanner Award for Excellence in Undergraduate Teaching. Dr. Cobb is also the recipient of fellowships and research grants from the American Philosophical Society, the Organization of American Historians, the Friends of the Princeton University Library, the Morris K. Udall Archives, the Newberry Library, the Carl Albert Congressional Research and Studies Center, and the University of North Carolina's Institute for the Arts and Humanities.

Dr. Cobb's publications include *Native Activism in Cold War America: The Struggle for Sovereignty*, winner of the inaugural Labriola Center American Indian National Book Award; *Beyond Red Power: American Indian Politics and Activism since 1900*; *Memory Matters*; a revised and expanded fourth edition of William T. Hagan's classic work *American Indians*; and *Say We Are Nations: Documents of Politics and Protest in Indigenous America since 1887*. He has made guest appearances on *Native America Calling* and *Sojourner Truth* and has contributed an essay on memory in *The Chronicle of Higher Education*. ■

ABOUT OUR PARTNER

Founded in 1846, the Smithsonian Institution is the world's largest museum and research complex, consisting of 19 museums and galleries, the National Zoological Park, and 9 research facilities. The total number of artifacts, works of art, and specimens in the Smithsonian's collections is estimated at 138 million. These collections represent America's rich heritage, art from across the globe, and the immense diversity of the natural and cultural world.

In support of its mission—the increase and diffusion of knowledge—the Smithsonian has embarked on four Grand Challenges that describe its areas of study, collaboration, and exhibition: Unlocking the Mysteries of the Universe, Understanding and Sustaining a Biodiverse Planet, Valuing World Cultures, and Understanding the American Experience. The Smithsonian's partnership with The Great Courses is an engaging opportunity to encourage continuous exploration by learners of all ages across these diverse areas of study.

This course, *Native Peoples of North America*, offers a multidisciplinary perspective on the experience of American Indians in the five centuries that have passed since two worlds collided in 1492. From complex interactions between Native communities and British colonists in Virginia and Massachusetts to 20th-century court battles over tribal sovereignty and religious freedom, the course tells stories of encounters and exchanges, negotiations and border crossings, accommodation and resistance. At its heart, though, it tells a story of Indigenous survival. It shows not only how Native peoples have persisted and adapted in the face of hardship, but also how they have made profound cultural contributions to America and the world. ■

TABLE OF CONTENTS

INTRODUCTION
Professor Biography i
Course Scope 1

LECTURE GUIDES

LECTURE 1
Native America: A Story of Survival............................. 4

LECTURE 2
The Columbian Exchange: New Worlds for All................... 12

LECTURE 3
The Native South and Southwest in the 1600s................... 20

LECTURE 4
Werowocomoco and Montaup in the 1600s..................... 28

LECTURE 5
Iroquoia and Wendake in the 1600s............................ 37

LECTURE 6
Indian-European Encounters, 1700–1750....................... 45

LECTURE 7
The Seven Years' War in Indian Country 53

LECTURE 8
The American Revolution through Native Eyes.................. 60

LECTURE 9
Indian Resistance in the Ohio Country 68

LECTURE 10
Indian Removal: Many Trails, Many Tears 75

LECTURE 11
Native Transformations on the Great Plains 82

LECTURE 12
Indians, Manifest Destiny, and Uncivil Wars 89

LECTURE 13
Native Resistance in the West, 1850s–1870s 97

LECTURE 14
The Last Indian Wars? 106

LECTURE 15
Challenging Assimilation and Allotment 114

LECTURE 16
American Indians and the Law, 1883–1903 122

LECTURE 17
The Ghost Dance and the Peyote Road 130

LECTURE 18
Native America in the Early 1900s 138

LECTURE 19
American Indians and World War I 146

LECTURE 20
Making a New Deal in Native America 154

LECTURE 21
American Indians and World War II 161

LECTURE 22
Indian Termination or Self-Determination? 169

LECTURE 23
Native Radicalism and Reform, 1969–1978. 177

LECTURE 24
Reasserting Rights and Tribal Sovereignty 185

SUPPLEMENTAL MATERIAL
Bibliography 193
Image Credits 205

NATIVE PEOPLES OF NORTH AMERICA

Scope:

For this course, The Great Courses has teamed with the Smithsonian Institution's National Museum of the American Indian and award-winning professor Daniel M. Cobb of the University of North Carolina at Chapel Hill to offer a multidisciplinary perspective on the peoples indigenous to North America from before contact with Europe to contemporary times.

Filled with images and artifacts from the famed Smithsonian collections, this 24-lecture course provides new perspectives on the historical and contemporary experiences of indigenous peoples. Rather than rehashing worn-out narratives of discovery, frontiers, conquest, and disappearance, it tells stories of encounters and exchanges, negotiations and border crossings, accommodation and resistance.

At its heart, though, rests a story of indigenous survival—what the associate curator of the National Museum of the American Indian, Paul Chaat Smith (Comanche), calls "one of the most extraordinary stories in human history."

The course begins with the origin stories that indigenous peoples and archaeologists have fashioned to explain the peopling of Native North America. From there, we explore the diverse culture areas of Native America prior to contact with Europe. In so doing, we gain an appreciation for how incredibly vibrant, dynamic, and interconnected a space it was. Places such as the Ozette, the Dalles, Chaco Canyon, Cahokia, and Head-Smashed-In reveal not a static "new world" existing outside of history but a cosmopolitan space of great antiquity that had seen the rise and fall of entire civilizations long before the arrival of Europeans.

Moving into the early colonial period, we explore how a complex process called the Columbian exchange created "new worlds for all" by transforming the lives of indigenous peoples and Europeans alike. Sixteenth- and seventeenth-century encounters are viewed through riveting case studies of Powhatan, Wampanoag, Iroquois, Wendat, post-Mississippian chiefdom, and Pueblo interactions with the English, French, and Spanish. In so doing, pivotal figures, including Powhatan, Pocahontas, Metacom, and Popé, are cast in an entirely new light.

We'll learn that, despite the pretentions of European "discoverers," Native America remained Native ground all through the 18th century; that is, Native peoples were, for the most part, in positions of power, and they meant to keep it that way. We'll explore how they maintained power in the context of case studies of the Iroquois Confederacy, the Lenape, the diverse Algonquian-speaking peoples of the Ohio River Valley, and the indigenous nations of the Arkansas River Valley, Southwest, and Pacific Northwest.

It's here that we will really begin to turn the standard narrative of American history on its head. A series of lectures takes familiar events that we often take for granted—the Seven Years' War, the American Revolution, the War of 1812, Cherokee removal, westward expansion, the Civil War, and the Indian Wars—and refashions them as struggles for continuing independence; unnatural quarrels; attempts to restore sacred power; nation-building campaigns; moments of profound cultural, social, and political transformation; and prophetic events. We look anew at well-known figures, such as Pontiac, Tecumseh, John Ross, Black Kettle, Sitting Bull, and Geronimo, and introduce many others you may never have heard of before.

Too often, American Indian history is treated as though it ended in 1890 with the horrific massacre of innocent Lakota men, women, and children at Wounded Knee. The last third of this course corrects this common misperception by exploring the many and varied ways that Native people navigated the extraordinary challenges of the late 19th and 20th centuries.

We will revisit the Ghost Dance and Wounded Knee, but we will also travel the Peyote Road. We will see how Native people sought to use the ideas and institutions of the majority society to knock the "pulverizing engine of progress" off its tracks. We'll learn about the unintended consequences of assimilation through the lives of returned students, artists, actors, athletes, and intellectuals during the early 20th century.

The story of survival, resistance, and renaissance is carried forward through engaging accounts of how Native people experienced both of the 20th century's world wars; moments of reform, such as the New Deal during the 1930s; and renewed assaults on tribal sovereignty during the Cold War era. Moving into the 1960s and 1970s, we will learn about how tribal leaders, young people, fishing-rights activists, and radicals articulated a vision of freedom predicated on the idea of self-determination and sovereignty.

And we conclude with a survey of how American Indians have tested and continue to test the limits of an inherent and enduring sovereignty in contemporary times. Here, we gain insights into critically important issues, such as gaming, repatriation, religious freedom, recognition, jurisdiction, and resource development.

All told, this course recounts an epic story of resistance and accommodation, persistence and adaption, extraordinary hardship and survival across more than 500 years of colonial encounter.

NATIVE AMERICA: A STORY OF SURVIVAL

Lecture 1

In the introductory text for "Our Peoples," one of the inaugural exhibits at the Smithsonian's National Museum of the American Indian in Washington DC, the curators drew a distinction between the past and history. "The past never changes," they observed. "But the way we understand it, learn about it, and know about it changes all the time." "Our Peoples" presented a version of American Indian history that countered popular narratives of victimization, defeat, and disappearance. In so doing, the curators, in collaboration with tribal communities, translated the events of the past into a different history—a chronicle of indigenous survival they aptly described as "one of the most extraordinary stories in human history." This course will explore that story.

Recovery and Renaissance

❖ Since the advent of colonialism in the late 15th century, American Indians repeatedly faced what seemed to be impossible odds, and throughout this history, non–Native Americans predicted that tribal lands, polities, and cultures would disappear. The impact of colonialism is still evident across Indian Country, but Native America has also experienced both recovery and a renaissance.

❖ This recovery and renaissance is rooted in a long tradition of resilience and perseverance, but it gained momentum in the second half of the 20th century, and it continues to this day.

❖ In fact, 567 tribal nations have a formal nation-to-nation relationship with the U.S. government. In 2010, there were 334 federal- and state-recognized American Indian reservations located in 35 states. The total landmass controlled by American Indians and Alaska Natives equaled approximately 100 million acres.

❖ There has also been a population recovery. According to the 2010 U.S. census, 5.2 million people identified as American Indian or Alaska Native. It's estimated that the number may increase to 8.6 million by 2050.

Tribes as Sovereign Nations

❖ At the heart of Native recovery and renaissance is sovereignty. Since the initial encounters with European colonial powers, tribes have been recognized as sovereign nations. And, upon its founding, the United States continued to recognize the political status of tribal nations.
  › This can be seen clearly in the 370 treaties with tribal nations that the United States signed and ratified between 1778 and 1871. Treaties are nation-to-nation agreements and considered under the U.S. Constitution to be "the supreme law of the land."
  › Treaties accomplished many things, such as establishing peace; defining boundaries; and affirming hunting, fishing, and water rights both on and off reservation lands. Often in return for land cessions, treaties obligated the federal government to provide health care, education, housing, and economic development.
  › What's more, treaties established a fiduciary or trust relationship, in which the federal government accepted the responsibility to assist tribes in the protection of their lands and resources, honor their treaty rights, and promote self-government and economic development.
  › It's absolutely essential to recognize that treaties didn't "give" Native nations anything—especially sovereignty. Rather, they acknowledged it.

❖ In its simplest form, we might think of sovereignty as the authority to self-govern. But *tribal* sovereignty is more than that. In fact, Lumbee legal scholar David Wilkins offers another definition of tribal sovereignty that is particularly illuminating:

> the spiritual, moral, and dynamic cultural force within a given tribal community empowering the group toward political, economic, and, most important, cultural integrity, and toward maturity in the group's relationships with its own members, with other peoples and their governments, and with the environment.

- This definition highlights the extraconstitutional and inherent nature of tribal sovereignty, affirming that it's something that can't be "granted" or "given" by someone else.

- Tribal sovereignty, then, is a generative force that manifests itself in any number of ways. For instance, tribal governments manifest sovereignty by:
  › Determining the form government should take
  › Establishing criteria for citizenship
  › Creating and exercising jurisdiction over civil and criminal laws
  › Taxing, licensing, and regulating business
  › Promoting economic development
  › Providing basic services, including health, housing, education, social welfare, law enforcement, and roads.

- Like the strengthening of tribal governments, the resurgent economies of many tribal nations speak to recovery and renaissance. For example, studies conducted in 2012 found that the 38 tribal nations in Oklahoma supported 87,700 jobs. In Washington, 29 tribal nations created 27,300 jobs in tribal government. These jobs produced $1.3 billion in employee wages that generated $255 million in state and local taxes annually.

Other Expressions of Sovereignty

- But sovereignty, as Wilkins suggests, isn't just about self-government and economic development. It also has a broader cultural dimension.

- In contemporary Native America, sovereignty expresses itself in education; in literature, art, architecture, music, and film; in the practice of traditional ecological knowledge and the recovery of foodways; in the revitalization of indigenous languages; in the reclamation of history; and in the tribal college movement and American Indian Studies programs.

❖ In a brilliant summary of where all these examples lead, the Comanche writer Paul Chaat Smith expressed the dynamism and diversity of contemporary Native America, Native nations, and Native people this way: "Modern American Indians are not shadows of their ancestors, but their equals."

❖ Without diminishing the fact that statistics on poverty; joblessness; and health, education, and income all point to profound ongoing challenges, it's worth asking: Why isn't Native America typically imagined as a place experiencing recovery and renaissance? Much of the answer resides in the power of history. History shapes memory, and memory shapes both the present and the future.

Historical Narrative of American Indians

- For a long time, non-Indians wrote as though American Indian history began in 1492—with the so-called discovery of the New World. In these works, indigenous people were portrayed as supporting actors in the story of the founding and expansion of America.

- At worst, Indians were cast as bloodthirsty savages—at best, as coconspirators in their own undoing or tragic heroes who valiantly resisted before accepting the inevitability of their demise. Either way, they eventually exited the stage.

- History, thus conceived, served as a powerful handmaiden of conquest. By writing Indians out of the past, this version of America's origin story denied Native people a present and a future.

- Perhaps the most emblematic work in this tradition is historian Frederick Jackson Turner's essay "The Significance of the Frontier in American History."
    - Jackson's 1893 essay defined the frontier as the "meeting point between savagery and civilization" and the source of the unique (and decidedly white) "American" character.
    - Turner bemoaned the fact that 400 years after "discovery," the frontier had finally closed—and with it, he surmised, came the end of Indian history.
    - Soon, Turner clearly believed, the "savage" Indians who had done so much to inspire the unique American spirit would be gone.
    - In truth, Turner didn't create this narrative so much as he canonized it. Indeed, as the scholar Philip Deloria notes, "This spatial reading of Indian history as a contest between the savage and the civilized has origins as old as European colonization." So, too, did the assumption that the narrative must end in physical conquest.

- Throughout the 17th to 19th centuries, non-Native historians wrote and rewrote the same history of inevitable conquest, though located in different times and places and involving different Native peoples. Such writing resulted in internalized ideas about the impossibility of Indians having a present, much less a future. By the late 19th and early 20th centuries, these messages about Indians and the end of Indian history were ubiquitous.

Counter-Narratives

- It's necessary, however, to balance the construction of this oppressive historical narrative with the creation of counter-narratives. We begin with the observation that there has never been a time when Native people were not the authors of their own histories.

- The oral traditions and histories found across indigenous cultures have always been a means of recording the past. "And," Deloria writes, "[Native people] have reshaped it in order to meet social, cultural, and political challenges."

- It's also true that on July 4, 1827, leaders of the Cherokee Nation opened a convention that led to the adoption of a constitution. Modeled on the U.S. and state constitutions, it reflected Cherokee values and was meant to protect Cherokee sovereignty.

- Moving forward in time, Native and non-Native scholars transformed history from within the academy during the second half of the 20th century. During the 1960s, the so-called New Indian History turned a critical eye toward celebratory conquest narratives and began to craft Indian-centered stories that recorded Native history from Native points of view.

- A number of scholars came together in March 1970 for the First Convocation of American Indian Scholars at Princeton University. Their goal was "to bring about a change in the way Native life in America was studied."

- The creation of new historical narratives developed unevenly, particularly in terms of the time periods on which they were focused. Most of the revisionist work from the 1970s through the 1990s, for instance, covered the 400 years of initial contact between Natives and newcomers and the end of the 19th century.

- Around the Columbian Quincentenary in 1992, a new interpretive framework focused on encounters emerged. Histories modeled on encounters supplanted worn-out narratives of discovery and conquest by emphasizing diplomacy, negotiation, and exchange.

- In so doing, the problematic concept of a rigid racially defined "frontier" gave way to dynamic conceptions of middle grounds, contact zones, edges, and borderlands.

- Strangely, though, few scholars had much to say about encounters that took place after 1900. Instead, historians typically imagined 20th-century American Indian history as being fundamentally different in nature from the more distant past.

- In recent years, scholars have challenged the drawing of sharp distinctions between the distant and more recent past. Yes, the balance of power shifted dramatically through the 19th and 20th centuries. But this shift amounted primarily to a change in the context of encounters between Natives and newcomers. It didn't bring an end to the encounters themselves.

- If 20th- and 21st-century encounters have remained a two-way street, then we can reimagine the last two centuries as a seamless part of one grand narrative.

- Frederick Jackson Turner and other frontier historians wanted people to believe that American Indian history had ended, that Native people would vanish, and that tribal sovereignty would disappear along with them. They turned the past into a history that served as a weapon of conquest in the 19th century and that serves as a roadblock to recovery and renaissance in Native America today.

- But the creation of new historical narratives can help to remove that roadblock. Indeed, recalling the words of Wilkins, we can now add the rewriting of the old master narrative as another manifestation of tribal sovereignty. This reassertion of sovereignty through the reclaiming of history seems especially poignant in the context of the books and articles authored by Native scholars—many of whom offer historical perspectives on their own families, communities, and nations.

- That's what this course is about. Like the "Our Peoples" exhibit and the work of scholars in the field of American Indian Studies, it's about translating the events of the past into a different history—a history of indigenous survival through more than 500 years of colonialism, one of the most extraordinary stories in human history.

Suggested Reading

Bruyneel, *The Third Space of Sovereignty.*

Denetdale, *Reclaiming Diné History.*

Harvard Project on American Indian Economic Development, *The State of the Native Nations.*

Klein, *Frontiers of Historical Imagination.*

Sleeper-Smith, Barr, O'Brien, Shoemaker, and Stevens, eds., *Why You Can't Teach United States History without American Indians.*

Smith, *Everything You Know about Indians Is Wrong.*

Vizenor, *Manifest Manners.*

Questions to Consider

1. How does the vibrancy of contemporary Native America complicate notions of discovery, frontiers, and the master narrative of American history?

2. How have Native and non-Native scholars challenged the old narratives of American Indian defeat and disappearance?

THE COLUMBIAN EXCHANGE: NEW WORLDS FOR ALL

Lecture 2

The Old World/New World binary that most of us take for granted is hopelessly Eurocentric. Embedded in it is the idea that "civilized Europe" discovered the "backward Americas" in 1492. Discovery is followed by "settlement," and settlement leads to the founding of new nations. This binary is the stepping-off point for America's master narrative. The truth of the matter is that both these worlds and all the peoples who lived in them were of great antiquity. Through contact, these old worlds became new to each other. Thus, in this lecture, we'll explore an era of mutual discovery and mutual transformations that, in the words of historian Colin Calloway, led to the creation of "new worlds for all."

Causes of Initial Contact
- The invasions of the Americas were sparked by the emergence of a new order in Europe. That order was founded on some old ideas, such as a crusading spirit that considered conquest over "infidels" to be part and parcel of glorifying God. The new order also featured some new elements, including innovations that made transoceanic voyages possible, the evolution of "national" geographical and political identities, and the rise of the theory of mercantilism, in which governments promoted trade to generate national wealth.

- These forces at work in Europe inspired the voyage that resulted in the geographical miscalculation that brought Columbus's ships not to India but to the island home of the Taíno in the Caribbean in 1492.
  - These same impulses prompted the sailing of English ships that the Mi'kmaq and Beothuk witnessed along the coast from present-day Maine to Nova Scotia five years later.

- Within the next three decades, Waccamaw, Lenape, Wampanoag, and Abenaki people along the coastline from the Carolinas to Newfoundland and Algonquian and Iroquoian people in the St. Lawrence River Valley traded and held council with explorers flying the fleur-de-lis.
- To the south, the Calusa and other Mississippian chiefdoms encountered Spanish conquistadors during the latter's expeditions into Florida in 1513. Indigenous people there, as well as in the Gulf Coast, Southwest, and Arkansas River Valley, dealt with waves of increasingly hostile Spaniards during the first decades of the 16th century.

❖ In some parts of the Americas, these initial contacts were the last time Indians would see European newcomers for 50 to 100 years. Elsewhere, the strangers established colonial settlements, seeking to extend political control over and economically exploit indigenous people and land.
- The Spanish secured a foothold at Saint Augustine in present-day Florida in 1565. Thirty-three years later, colonists entered Pueblo homelands throughout the Rio Grande Valley in New Mexico.
- Along the Atlantic coast, in present-day North Carolina, a group of English colonists founded a small settlement on Croatan and Secotan land. This ill-fated venture was followed by the founding of permanent colonies within the Powhatan Confederacy at Jamestown, in what is today Virginia, in 1607; within the Wampanoag Confederacy at Plymouth in 1620; and at Massachusetts Bay in 1630.
- Meanwhile, French traders, trappers, priests, and colonists established settlements among the Indians of the St. Lawrence River Valley between 1603 and 1615.

The Columbian Exchange: Plants and Animals

❖ Scholars use the term "Columbian exchange" to describe the driving force behind the creation of "new worlds for all." Following scholar Alfred Crosby, the term can be defined as the transference of plants, animals, and diseases among the Americas, Eurasia, and Africa unleashed by Christopher Columbus's geographical miscalculation. The process and consequences of this convergence are mind-boggling in their complexity.

- In terms of plants, Europeans brought with them everything from grains, such as white rice, wheat, barley, oats, and rye, to vegetables, including turnips, onions, cabbages, and lettuce. They also carried cuttings for fruit trees, including peaches, pears, and apples.
    - Of course, Europeans accelerated the transformative impact of plants by clearing fields and cutting down forests, a practice in which Native people also engaged.
    - The transformations that attended the exchange of plants did not go only in one direction. Indigenous peoples introduced non-Natives to corn, white potatoes, sweet potatoes, and manioc or cassava, as well as peanuts, tomatoes, cocoa, squash, pumpkins, pineapples, papaya, and avocados.
    - Consider, too, the impact of nonfood plants. Tobacco—a crop that would be among the first to make colonization viable and profitable because of its popularity in Europe—was indigenous to the Americas.

- A second component of the Columbian exchange was the exchange of animals, which proved no less stunning.
    - As early as 1493—with Columbus's return voyage to the Caribbean—Europeans brought with them a host of animals that indigenous people had never seen before, including donkeys, goats, sheep, chickens, pigs, and cattle. Perhaps most startling would have been the horse, which dwarfed any animal that Native peoples had domesticated at the time of contact.
    - These animals contributed to the remaking of indigenous American landscapes and lives—sometimes making life easier and, at other times, introducing new hardships. Consider, for instance, the rise of the Horse Nations, such as the Lakota, Comanche, and Apache on the Plains, during the 18th century. What so many people take to be the quintessence of "Indian-ness"—the equestrian cultures of the Plains—is, in fact, a product of the Columbian exchange.
    - Native communities successfully integrated new animals that came to form central parts of their identities. As with plants, however, the

Europeans brought many animals, birds, and insects with them, including black rats, starlings, and honeybees.

impact of new animals wasn't always beneficial. The introduction of sheep and cattle—both as grazers and as excreters—had a significant impact on native flora and contributed to ecological changes across the continent.

> Further, some of these four-legged newcomers reproduced with remarkable speed, especially in the absence of human or animal predators. When Hernando de Soto began his exploration in 1539, he brought with him 13 pigs. By the time of his death three years later, that number had grown to about 700. The consequences for indigenous people were destabilizing and often destructive.

> Among the most important animals to make the Atlantic crossing from North America to Europe were cod and beaver. Along the Grand Banks of Newfoundland, non-Native fishers caught and cured tons of cod, an essential part of European diets. Beaver pelts were highly sought after because of their warmth, texture, and durability.

The Columbian Exchange: Disease

- The transformative impact of plants and animals paled in comparison to that of the Columbian exchange's third major component: disease, as close to a one-way street as might be found in the exchange.

- Before 1492, there were almost no infectious diseases in the Americas that were not also found in Eurasia and Africa. However, nonindigenous traders, fishers, explorers, conquistadors, missionaries, and settlers brought with them smallpox, malaria, yellow fever, measles, cholera, typhus, bubonic plague, whooping cough, and other sicknesses.

- Each of these triggered what is known as a virgin soil epidemic; that is, through the Columbian exchange, Europeans unleashed diseases that had never been seen before and to which Native peoples had no immunity. The consequences were devastating.

- Indeed, disease served as an epidemiological vanguard for colonization all through the Americas, often wiping out entire villages or sending them into diaspora before a non-Native person was even seen.

- Consider, as one example, the conquest of the Mexica, the Mesoamerican people commonly—but inaccurately—referred to as Aztecs.
  > Smallpox, once introduced to the mainland in 1519, spread through central Mexico with devastating consequences.
  > In short order, it reached Tenochtitlán, the capital city of the Mexica, and decimated the population. The Spanish conquistador Hernán Cortés viciously finished the job in 1521.

❖ Disease worked its cruel way across Native North America, as well. The French established the cities of Montreal and Quebec on the ruins of Hochelaga and Stadacona, respectively. Both of these villages were surrounded by vast fields of corn and heavily populated by St. Lawrence Iroquoians when they came into contact with French explorers in 1535 and 1536. When French colonists returned 70 years later, they were deserted.

Hernán Cortés

❖ All through the mid-16th and early 17th centuries, epidemics raced through Indian villages along the St. Lawrence River Valley and into New England. Mortality rates varied but often exceeded 75 percent. In addition, outbreaks of smallpox, cholera, measles, and other diseases repeatedly crashed through indigenous communities along the Eastern Seaboard and through the Southeast.

❖ Epidemics propelled entire communities into diaspora. In the Native South, for instance, some coastal and Piedmont communities dispersed into the interior and reconstituted themselves as new people. As Native peoples reconstituted their communities, Europeans filled the power vacuums created by disease. They often looked at the devastation wrought by disease as confirmation of their right to the land.

Other Aspects of the Columbian Exchange
❖ Bodily and genetic exchange were also part of the Columbian exchange. Virtually all of the early Europeans explorers wrote of taking indigenous

people (willingly or unwillingly) back to Europe as objects of curiosity or, from Native vantage points, as captives, slaves, or sometimes emissaries.

- ❖ The introduction of cotton and sugar to North America carried devastating consequences for indigenous people and Africans, many of whom were taken into bondage and forced to cultivate these crops.

- ❖ The presence of European slavers, demographic collapse, competition over trade, and increased warfare intensified and redefined existing indigenous practices of captive taking and slavery, as well.

- ❖ To further complicate our understanding of the Columbian exchange's transformative consequences, we might consider, too, the genetic exchange born of sexual relationships between Natives and newcomers, as well as the transference of beliefs, political ideals, technologies, and everyday material objects, from glass beads and mirrors to copper pots, knives, awls, and guns.

- ❖ We might also contemplate the exchange of ideas about the nature of land and its resources, what gives land value and how people should relate to it. In fact, this exchange of ideas is far from over.

Contact between Two Worlds

- ❖ In this lecture, we've seen how two worlds of great antiquity, each unaware of the other for thousands of years, suddenly became new to the other. And we've seen how contact inaugurated an era of mutual discovery and exchange that created "new worlds for all."

- ❖ We should keep in mind, however, that much of what we imagine as "new" might have been thought of by indigenous contemporaries more simply as "next." After all, Native communities were already practiced in the arts of dealing with people unlike themselves, the exchange of material and nonmaterial things across vast trade networks, and innovations to their ways of life.

❖ As they had been doing for thousands of years before the advent of the Columbian exchange, indigenous people would make sense of these "nextcomers" on their own terms. And, in so doing, they would seek to restore order as two worlds of great antiquity collided.

Suggested Reading

Calloway, *New Worlds for All*.

Crosby, *The Columbian Exchange*.

Mann, *1491*.

Mann, *1493*.

Richter, *Before the Revolution*.

Questions to Consider

1. Why do you think Europe and Asia are typically cast as the Old World and North America as the New World? How does the idea of "new worlds for all" challenge that binary?

2. How does imagining Europeans as "nextcomers" rather than newcomers change the way we think about Native America before and after the onset of the Columbian exchange?

THE NATIVE SOUTH AND SOUTHWEST IN THE 1600S

Lecture 3

We'll begin this lecture by surveying the indigenous worlds that emerged from the decline of the Mississippian tradition in the Southeast and the Ancestral Pueblos in the Southwest. Then, to understand how Natives and newcomers attempted to pull each other into their worlds, we'll focus on case studies involving Hernando de Soto's entrada, or expedition, through the Southeast between 1539 and 1542 and the Pueblo Revolt or War for Independence in the Southwest more than a century later.

Inhabitants of the Southeast

- The inhabitants of the Southeast were ancestors of Siouan, Iroquoian, and Muskogean language speakers, as well as speakers of other distinct languages. Agriculture predominated in the region, supplemented by hunting, gathering, and fishing. Families were typically matrilineal and matrilocal. The common practice of clan exogamy—marrying outside of one's clan—served to bind people in the region together by extending kinship ties. Hereditary rulers and hierarchical political structures were common in the region.

- The Spanish, who had already devastated the Taíno in the Caribbean, the Mexica in Mesoamerica, and the Inca in Peru, invaded this southeastern world during the fourth decade of the 16th century.

- What drove the Spanish? To answer that question, we need to consider the three pillars of Spanish conquest.
    - The first was a lust for battle, which they rationalized in a document called El Requerimiento, or "The Requirement." Devised by Spanish

jurists and theologians in the early 16th century, the Requerimiento announced that God had created all men, that all men were bound to obey God's will, and that the Spaniards were "dutifully expressing God's will by subduing non-Christians and reclaiming them for the Catholic Church." Conquistadors gave Indians a choice: submit or die.

› Implicit in the Requerimiento were the second and third pillars of Spanish conquest. The second pillar was God—that is, the Spanish desire to convert people they considered to be "heathen savages."

› The third pillar was gold or, more broadly conceived, the generation of wealth from the exploitation of indigenous land and labor.

Hernando de Soto's Entrada

* The capital of the chiefdom of Cofitachequi was located along the Wateree River near present-day Camden, South Carolina. It was probably the principal town within a paramount chiefdom, which consisted of an alliance among several simple chiefdoms of four to seven neighboring villages.

* In May 1540, the niece of the paramount chief, a woman the Spanish called the Lady of Cofitachequi, ceremoniously crossed the river, where she received Hernando de Soto and his band of

Hernando de Soto

Spanish newcomers. By that time, the Cofitachequi already possessed Spanish trade goods, and the Lady had assuredly heard stories about them.

- Over the previous 12 months, Soto, 600 soldiers, 24 priests, 100 slaves, and a number of ferocious Irish wolfhounds had blundered and plundered their way through present-day Florida and Georgia in search of riches equal to those found in Mexico and Peru. Along the way, they killed, kidnapped, raped, and enslaved, sending shockwaves through surrounding areas.

- The Lady of Cofitachequi also knew that the newcomers brought strange sicknesses with them, plagues that led to the abandonment of several nearby towns. But when she crossed the river to greet the bearded warrior with gifts, she was attempting to incorporate him into a Cofitachequi world on Cofitachequi terms.

- Probably already knowing the answer, she began by asking Soto whether he intended peace or war. Acting like a conqueror, rather than the potential ally the Cofitachequi hoped for, Soto proceeded to make a list of demands, including the source of the pearls she had given him. She told him where to go to find the riches he sought.

- Soto and his men plundered a mortuary temple and took pounds of pearls off the bodies of the dead, as well as European trade goods. Unsatisfied, the Spaniards returned to Cofitachequi and took captives and hostages, including the Lady, before continuing into present-day North Carolina.

- Soto and his men proceeded into Tennessee and northern Georgia, where they spent 100 days plundering and terrorizing Coosa, another wealthy paramount chiefdom. In Alabama and Tennessee, the Spaniards attacked virtually all the palisaded towns they encountered.

- As had happened previously, news of the invaders traveled ahead of them and shaped the approaches Native people adopted.

- > In October 1540, for instance, the Tuscaloosa in Mabila, a chiefdom near modern-day Selma, Alabama, welcomed the Spaniards much as the Lady of Cofitachequi had done. But this time, several thousand warriors concealed themselves in Mabila houses and struck hard at the Spaniards.
  - > The Spaniards delivered a devastating counterattack, slaughtering thousands of Tuscaloosas and burning the town to the ground.

- In May 1541—two years into the expedition—Soto's men crossed the Mississippi. Now, their mission turned from seeking gold to an increasingly desperate search for a route home. Along the way, the Native peoples took every opportunity to defend their homelands against the Spaniards by adopting guerilla tactics.

- In the Arkansas River Valley, during the winter of 1541–1542, Soto's desperation deepened. On the brink of death, the conquistador ordered one last assault on a town the Spaniards called Anlico. On foot and horseback, with wolfhounds by their side, they slaughtered more than 100 people.

- On May 21, 1542, Soto died of a fever somewhere near the confluence of the Arkansas and Mississippi Rivers. His soldiers paddled his body to the middle of the Mississippi and sent it to the bottom, where it could never be found. Their action speaks volumes about their knowledge of what they had done.

- When the Spaniards returned about 20 years later, the colonists found what scholars refer to as a shatter zone. This was a large region of instability throughout eastern North America from the late 1500s to the early 1700s, resulting from the collapse of the Mississippian chiefdoms and the introduction of European disease.

- At the same time, the Southeast was being born anew as Native people rebuilt their towns, replanted their fields, and replenished their storehouses. The survivors of collapse restored order in the shatter zone by producing the societies known as the Creek, Choctaw, Chickasaw, Cherokee, and Catawba.

The Pueblo Revolt or War for Independence

- The events that culminated in the Pueblo Revolt or War for Independence in 1680 represent another attempt by indigenous people to restore order.

- The 16th-century Pueblo world was the product of great changes, many of which had been inaugurated by the outmigration of the Ancestral Pueblos by 1300. This, in turn, led to their merging with surrounding Indian communities in all directions. By the 1500s, the Pueblo world included a number of towns, or pueblos, along the Rio Grande and elsewhere. These people shared lifeways but spoke six mutually unintelligible languages.

- The Pueblo built a rich life rooted in sedentary villages supported by agriculture, but they were connected to a wider world. Trade among the Diné, or Navajo; the Apache; and the Pueblo included goods, as well as ideas, architectural forms, and ceremonial practices.

- In 1540, Francisco Vásquez de Coronado came to the pueblo of Hawikuh with an army. His expedition was met by 200 Zuni warriors—and a cornmeal line. The cornmeal line symbolically closed the road leading to Hawikuh and was meant to convey that Zuni ceremonies were in progress and not to be interrupted. Here, we see another example of how Native people attempted to engage newcomers in their accustomed ways.

- Coronado ignored the Zunis' gesture and began a three-year campaign moving from pueblo to pueblo—then onto the Plains and back again—wreaking havoc in search of gold.

- The first attempt to colonize the Pueblo world began 50 years later, when Juan de Oñate arrived to establish a region the Spanish called "New Mexico." Once again, the invaders met the Pueblos with violence.

Local Pueblo communities held ceremonies in plazas and *kivas*—semi-subterranean structures that, in their architectural form, reflected Pueblo stories of emergence from a world below.

❖ Once they had established a foothold, Spanish colonial authorities began generating wealth by exploiting Pueblo land and labor through the encomienda and repartimiento systems.
  › Through encomienda, the holders of Spanish land grants (encomenderos) were given authority to demand labor and tribute from the Indians who lived on or near their plantations. In return, the encomenderos were expected to instruct Native workers on Christianity and, often, how to read and write.
  › In 1542, the Spanish began replacing the encomienda system with repartimiento, meaning "partition" or "distribution." It imposed forced—albeit paid—labor on indigenous populations.

❖ Through the early 17th century, the systems controlling the land and labor of indigenous people became increasingly oppressive. Meanwhile, colonial authorities imposed a governance structure that disempowered traditional Pueblo leaders, and Franciscan missionaries grew ever-more hostile toward Pueblo religious practices.

- By the mid-1600s, the Rio Grande Valley was also struggling with disease and drought. The Pueblo people suffered massive losses relative to their small population, declining from 40,000 to 17,000 between 1638 and 1670.

- The Pueblo social order had fallen apart and needed to be restored in order for their rituals to work and for life to continue. To restore harmony and balance, Pueblo caciques, or chiefs, led public performances of prayers, dances, and ceremonies. The Spanish responded with whipping, castration, rape, and sodomy.

- Matters reached the breaking point in 1675, when 47 Tewa medicine men were punished for performing traditional dances and ceremonies in public. Three were executed, one committed suicide, and the rest were imprisoned and sold into slavery.
  > Among them was Popé, a San Juan Pueblo, who laid the foundation for an ambitious pan-Pueblo rebellion against Spanish colonial oppression.
  > Joined by Diné and Apache allies, the Pueblo launched coordinated attacks on August 10, 1680. The violence resulted in the deaths of about 400 colonists and 20 friars.

- Ultimately, Santa Fe became the site of a final siege. After nine days, the Spaniards escaped and withdrew from New Mexico. From the perspective of many Pueblo participants, "God and Santa Maria" were now dead, but the Pueblos were unable to restore the entirety of the preexisting social order. Rather than harmony and balance, the succeeding years saw continued drought, pestilence, hunger, and political turmoil.

- Between 1692 and 1698, the Spanish returned—with a vengeance. At Santa Fe in December 1693, they executed 70 Pueblo men and distributed about 400 Indian women and children as slaves to colonists.

❖ The Pueblo struggle for independence resulted in reconquest—but it was far from over. Across the 16th- and 17th-century Southeast and Southwest, Native people tried to pull newcomers into their worlds on terms of their own making. They did so only to find that the leaders of these bewildering bands of Europeans refused to reciprocate their gifts. Yet Native peoples in the Southeast and Southwest endured. They named the conqueror, but they did not accept the name "conquered."

Suggested Reading

Ethridge and Shuck-Hall, eds., *Mapping the Mississippian Shatter Zone.*

Hudson, *Conversations with the High Priest of Coosa.*

———, *Knights of Spain, Warriors of the Sun.*

Knaut, *The Pueblo Revolt of 1680.*

Sando, *Pueblo Nations.*

Questions to Consider

1. In what ways do the two case studies—Hernando de Soto's entrada and the Pueblo Revolt or War for Independence—shed light on the idea that Columbus Day might be understood as time for mourning rather than celebration?

2. What do these two case studies tell us about how Native peoples made sense of European newcomers? How do they challenge the idea that Indians were overwhelmed by their presence?

WEROWOCOMOCO AND MONTAUP IN THE 1600S

Lecture 4

Everyday objects, such as brass arrowheads, earrings, linen shirts, and glass bottles, can tell us a great deal about early encounters between Natives and newcomers. What at first glance might appear to be a random mix of trade goods is, in fact, material evidence of a search for common ground. These objects also illustrate that the search for common ground has never been a one-way street; in fact, these objects tell stories of mutual incorporation and transformation that left no one unchanged. In this lecture, we'll build on the stories told by material objects as we explore the search for common ground in the Native Northeast from first contact through the end of the 17th century.

Werowocomoco

- ❖ Located on the York River in the Chesapeake, Werowocomoco served as the home of Powhatan, the paramount chief of the Powhatan Confederacy. Spanning 6,000 square miles, the Powhatan Confederacy included perhaps 15,000 Algonquian-speaking people from 30 distinct groups.

- ❖ As the paramount chief, Powhatan maintained power in this region through district chiefs and viceroys. Powhatan's emissaries collected tribute in the form of venison, deer hides, corn, strings of pearls, and shell beads.

- ❖ Given this system of political administration and tribute, the term "confederacy" is a bit misleading. In reality, many of the districts Powhatan controlled were created and sustained through intimidation, force, and even conquest. And some peoples, such as the Chickahominy and Monacan, refused to submit to Powhatan.

- Nonetheless, by the time John Smith and a small group of English settlers ventured into the Chesapeake Bay to establish Jamestown in 1607, just 12 miles from Werowocomoco, Powhatan held sway over much of Tidewater Virginia. Of course, his initial goal was to bring the colonists into his world on his terms.

- In December 1607, Powhatan had Smith and his exploratory party captured and brought to his longhouse in Werowocomoco. Powhatan then orchestrated a ritual of incorporation, acting out a hypothetical situation whereby Smith could have been killed but wasn't.
    - By having his daughter Pocahontas throw her body across Smith's, Powhatan symbolically took pity on him. In other words, he had no intention of killing Smith—not at that point, anyway.
    - Instead, Powhatan meant for this ritual to establish his authority over Smith and the newcomers. Powhatan believed that he had incorporated the English as subordinates, just as he had other Native communities throughout the region.

Pocahontas

- As soon as the cultivation of tobacco made it possible for increased settlement in the James River Valley in Virginia, colonists began pressing for (or simply taking) Indian land.

- Pocahontas, perhaps only 12 years old at the time, was in the thick of this, tasked with keeping the peace. She conveyed food, gifts, and important messages between the English and the Powhatan. She even negotiated the release of Powhatan prisoners held by the colonists, while shielding Englishmen from her father's wrath.

- In so doing, she risked her own life to preserve both the Virginia Colony and the Powhatan Confederacy. In her search for common ground, Pocahontas imagined a world in which each could exist.

Pocahontas memorial in Jamestown

- Yet contests over land erupted in war in 1610. Fighting did not end until Pocahontas was captured and taken hostage by the English and their Native allies in the spring of 1613. Peace was made when Pocahontas married colonist John Rolfe in 1614.

- Amid simmering hostilities, the Virginia Company struck upon the idea of bringing Pocahontas, John Rolfe, and their infant son, Thomas, back to England as a way to promote the colony. The family arrived in England in June 1616, and Pocahontas was received by King James I.

- In the spring of 1617, plans were made for a return trip to Virginia. But Pocahontas took ill while in London and died—at age 22—on the way home, perhaps of pneumonia or tuberculosis.

- In the final analysis, Powhatan's daughter was not merely a princess but an intermediary. Her life was devoted to pulling the English into a Powhatan world on Powhatan terms—terms that imagined the land could be shared. Unfortunately, the peace between the English and the Powhatan Confederacy did not survive her passing.

- Powhatan, too, died in 1618. And continuing conflict over the land—exacerbated by the spread of tobacco cultivation, land enclosure, and the destruction wrought by wandering cattle and foraging pigs—precipitated intense conflict. This was followed in 1622 and, again, in 1644 by brutally destructive wars.
    - Powhatan's successor and brother, Opechancanough, was captured in the wake of the latter war, put in a cage for the residents of Jamestown to see, and finally, shot in the back.
    - Although he clearly wanted to avoid such violence, Powhatan had foreseen these events for what they were: products of the inability of the English to forge the mutual and reciprocal ties necessary to establishing common ground.

Montaup

- Montaup was a Pokanoket village located in the heart of the Wampanoag Confederacy in present-day Rhode Island. Here, we see three similar themes:
  - Attempts by Natives and newcomers to pull each other into their worlds on their own terms
  - A cycle of diplomacy, exchange, conflict, violence, and concession
  - Renewed attempts on the part of indigenous people to reestablish common ground in a world transformed by settler colonialism.

- By the time the Pilgrims had established a presence at Plymouth late in 1620, the Native peoples of New England had been hammered by epidemics that may have wiped out 90 percent of the population.

- The Wampanoags had reconstituted themselves as a loose confederacy, led by a Pokanoket man named Massasoit. In the spring of 1621, Massasoit entered a treaty of friendship, mutual defense, and economic interdependency with the Pilgrims. At the outset, the treaty was beneficial to everyone. The Puritans gained protection, influence, and an important trade partner. The Wampanoags secured an ally against their rivals, such as the Narragansetts.

- Massasoit and the Wampanoag Confederacy prospered in the years that followed. Driving the wealth was an influx of trade items, particularly wampum—beads fashioned from whelk and quahog shells. Although already deeply woven into the fabric of Native lives, after contact, wampum took on new meaning as a form of currency.

- Massasoit managed to maintain Wampanoag sovereignty, but this became a more delicate balance with the added presence of the Massachusetts Bay Colony, which precipitated a large influx of settlers after its founding in 1630. To Massasoit and other Native people, perhaps the most challenging new influence was the Pilgrims' conception of God.

› Puritans believed that the world in which the Native people lived was evil—which, by extension, meant that Native people themselves were evil.
› They also believed that it was their mission to redeem this fallen land by constructing what Massachusetts Bay Governor John Winthrop called a "City upon a Hill." If world salvation required the dispossession and death of Indian people, so be it.

The Pequot War

❖ The Pequot War, which erupted in the Connecticut River Valley in 1636 and spread eastward, suggested how difficult the situation had become for Massasoit. The war grew out of a number of factors, among them land, trade, and the power vacuum left by epidemics.

❖ The fighting climaxed in 1637, when the English—along with Mohegan and Narragansett allies—marched on a Pequot village along the Mystic River. Upon surrounding and setting fire to the palisaded village, the contest swiftly devolved into slaughter.

❖ At the Treaty of Hartford the following year, the Europeans took from the Pequot not only their land and sovereignty but also the name Pequot, the use of which was outlawed.

❖ Massasoit's son Wamsutta became sachem in 1661 and began selling land to pacify the colonists. But rumors swirled that he intended to wage war. Plymouth authorities responded by sending an armed party to escort Wamsutta to a meeting; he died on the return trip.

❖ A younger brother, Metacom, now inherited an impossible situation. Amid continuing settler encroachment, Plymouth Colony authorized the purchase of additional lands from any Indian willing to sell. At the same time, the English extended their legal authority over the Wampanoag. In 1671, Metacom was forced to relinquish some of his people's guns and was expected to submit to colonial authority.

- War, triggered by a complicated series of events, erupted in the summer of 1675.
  - Over the previous winter, a Christian Indian named John Sassamon, who served as an aide to Metacom, seems to have conveyed to the colonial governors the Wampanoag sachem's plan to launch an intertribal assault.
  - Sassamon was found dead shortly afterward. Colonial authorities apprehended three Wampanoags, charged them with murder, and executed them.

- The Mohegan then allied with the English. The Narragansett tried to remain neutral, only to be attacked and driven back into an alliance with the Wampanoag. Meanwhile, Metacom's forces launched attacks against 52 English towns throughout the region, killing about 2,500 people. In return, the English and their Indian allies burned Wampanoag villages.

- Ultimately, Metacom's alliance fell apart. In the summer of 1676, a force consisting of colonists and their Indian allies captured and killed Metacom. His death effectively brought an end to military resistance in New England and dealt a tremendous blow to tribal sovereignty throughout the region.

The Powhatan People

- In Werowocomoco, things were falling apart for the Powhatan people, as well. Thomas Rolfe—the son of Pocahontas—had returned to Virginia in 1640. He cultivated tobacco on Powhatan lands and, in so doing, contributed to the colonization of them.

- After Opechancanough's murder in 1646, Virginia entered into a peace treaty that (ironically) defined the last vestiges of the Powhatan Confederacy as tributaries; they were increasingly subjected to English law.

- The remaining Chesapeake tribes found themselves caught in the middle of a dispute remembered as Bacon's Rebellion in 1675 and 1676.

Powhatan Indian Village Home

They, like the Wampanoag, were forced to grapple with the disastrous consequences.

The Search for Common Ground

- Although war was endemic in the Northeast during the 17th century, the views from Werowocomoco and Montaup suggest that it wasn't inevitable. Moreover, the actions taken by Native people, such as Powhatan, Pocahontas, Massasoit, and Metacom, show that the story of war is not the only one in need of telling.

- As with the everyday objects mentioned at the beginning of this lecture, their lives tell stories of a search for common ground, of mutual incorporation and transformation.

› By extending kinship ties, engaging in trade, and establishing relationships of mutuality and reciprocity, Native people across the Northeast attempted to pull Europeans into their worlds on terms of their own making.
› Europeans—in this instance, the English—simultaneously attempted to do the same—but the world they envisioned was less tolerant. There really wasn't a future for Native people in the Puritans' "City upon a Hill."

Suggested Reading

Lepore, *The Name of War.*

Mandell, *King Philip's War.*

Richter, *Facing East from Indian Country,* chaps. 1–4.

Rountree, *The Powhatan Indians of Virginia.*

Townsend, *Pocahontas and the Powhatan Dilemma.*

Questions to Consider

1. Why do you think the popular narratives of Pocahontas as either a love interest or as a savior are so tenacious?
2. The Powhatan, Wampanoag, and English attempted to pull one another into their worlds as they understood them to be. Were conflict and war inevitable outcomes of this process?

IROQUOIA AND WENDAKE IN THE 1600S

Lecture 5

In this lecture, we'll explore how Native people in the Northeast attempted to incorporate European newcomers into their worlds on terms of their own making from contact through the end of the 17th century—how they tried to establish and maintain a "measured separatism" even as their lives became ever more intertwined. We'll begin with an overview of the St. Lawrence Lowlands and Great Lakes–Riverine areas to get a sense of how diverse this vast region was at the time of contact. Then, we'll focus on the Wendat and Iroquois and their encounters with the newcomers to understand in greater depth how Native people transformed the European colonial project, even as they were being transformed by it.

St. Lawrence Lowlands and Great Lakes–Riverine Regions

❖ The St. Lawrence Lowlands stretch from southern Ontario in present-day Canada through upstate New York and across the St. Lawrence and Susquehanna River valleys. Along the St. Lawrence River from the Atlantic coast to Lake Ontario were Northern Iroquoian speakers, such as the St. Lawrence Iroquoians, the Iroquois, Wendat, Wenro, Petun, Neutral, and Susquehannock, as well as Algonquian language speakers, including the Algonquin.

❖ The Great Lakes–Riverine area includes all the Great Lakes and reaches down to what is today referred to as the Ohio River Valley. Most of the people in this region, including the Anishinaabeg, Odawa, Myaamia, Illinois, Shawnee, Ho-Chunk, and Menominee, spoke languages from the Algonquian or Siouan language families.

The Wendat and Iroquois

- The Iroquois and Wendat are both confederacies composed of distinct but linguistically related peoples.

- The Iroquois, also known collectively as the Iroquois Confederacy, the Haudenosaunee, and the People of the Longhouse, occupied an extensive area in what is today upstate New York, bordered by the Mohawk and Genesee River valleys. Moving from west to east, the Iroquois Confederacy included the Seneca, Cayuga, Onondaga, Oneida, and Mohawk.

- The Wendat, whose name means "Islanders" or "Dwellers on a Peninsula," lived in a more circumscribed space at the southeastern edge of Lake Huron's Georgian Bay in present-day Ontario. They called their homeland Wendake.

- The Wendat and Iroquois had much in common. They spoke languages that belonged to the Northern Iroquoian language family and practiced similar lifeways. For instance, both the Iroquois and Wendat lived in sedentary villages supported by a mixed economy of agriculture, fishing, hunting, and gathering. Their farming practices rested on sophisticated knowledge of genetic engineering and literally reshaped the land.

- Social organization was another area of commonality between the Iroquois and Wendat. Women were the primary agriculturalists, and—because they cultivated the land—they owned it, in a sense. This economic power translated into political power. Matrilineality, for instance, meant that one's identity was rooted in the mother's clan, and the right to lead rested on the authority of clan mothers. Men, in contrast, hunted, fished, traded, and waged war. With the support of clan mothers, they represented their people in the context of village, national, and international politics.

People of the Longhouse

- As mentioned, the five nations of the Iroquois Confederacy referred to themselves as the People of the Longhouse. Longhouses were impressive structures. Bent saplings provided the frames, and sheets of elm bark formed the outer shell. They were often 20 feet tall, 25 feet wide, and averaged from 80 to 100 feet long.

- Iroquois villages, although they varied in size, might consist of 30 to 150 longhouses, which were arranged in parallel rows—lying within 2 to 16 acres and often surrounded by wooden palisades—and provided shelter for up to 1,500 residents.

- The interior spatial geography of longhouses reveals their deeper cultural significance. The inside of each longhouse was divided into compartments that ran along either side of a center corridor. Members of nuclear families (which formed extended matrilineal families) lived in each compartment and shared a fire with the family directly across from them.

- This arrangement is meaningful. As historian Daniel Richter puts it: "The organization of physical space … embodied an ethic of sharing and reciprocity between kin groups." In fact, the entire Iroquois Confederacy was imagined as a longhouse.

Iroquois Longhouse

- Longhouses also served as the primary places of residence for the Wendat. And as with the Iroquois, Wendat longhouses reflected the values and patterns of social organization.

The Iroquois, Wendat, and European Contact

- Although the Iroquois and Wendat had much in common, not all was peaceful between them. In fact, hostilities between the Iroquois Confederacy and surrounding peoples, including the Wendat, were escalating just as Europeans began establishing their presence along the Eastern Seaboard.

- Led by Jacques Cartier, the French initially explored the St. Lawrence River Valley during the 1530s and early 1540s. Rumors of great riches carried them to the St. Lawrence Iroquoian villages of Stadacona and Hochelaga.

- The French navigator Samuel de Champlain followed in 1603. However, where Cartier had found miles of crops and orchards, Champlain witnessed devastation—the consequences of disease and intensifying intertribal warfare.

- To promote trade and compete with the Dutch, Champlain forged alliances.
    - The Innu to the north, the Algonquin along the St. Lawrence River, and the Wendat around the Great Lakes became intermediaries in a trade network that extended into modern-day northern Ontario.
    - To the south, the Neutral provided access to tobacco, wampum, and other marine shells. To the west, Odawa routes reached into the Prairie Plains and brought forth bison skins and catlinite, (pipestone) a malleable brownish-red clay used to make ceremonial objects.
    - Wendake was the center of this vast trade network, and the Wendat language served as the lingua franca for much of the region—even among speakers of Algonquian languages.
    - In fact, what the French liked to imagine as their North American "empire," was, in fact, dependent on centuries-old indigenous trade networks and the maintenance of good relations with the tribal

nations that controlled them. This is but one example of how the Wendat and the Iroquois transformed European colonialism, even as their lives were being transformed by it.

* Given intensifying hostilities with the Iroquois and a desire for trade goods, Wendat civil leaders forged political and military alliances with the French. Following an early alliance against the Mohawk, the French continued to meet Native expectations for diplomatic protocol, from patterns of speech to the giving of gifts. In so doing, the French acknowledged the idea of "measured separatism."

* Another example of mutual transformation can be found in religion. In 1633, for instance, Champlain made the continuation of trade with the Wendat contingent on their accepting Jesuit missionaries in their villages. Although the Wendat accepted the presence of missionaries, they did so on Wendat terms. The Wendat, like other Native people, indigenized Christianity or, at least, approached it in a way that did not necessarily conflict with their own conceptions of the sacred.

Mourning Wars

* Although the Jesuits met with little success initially, the cataclysms that visited Wendake during the 1630s and 1640s made them more open to Christianity. Between 1634 and 1640, the Wendat population was cut in half by a series of epidemics. But far more devastating than disease to the Wendat were escalating mourning wars and, by midcentury, the Beaver Wars with the Iroquois.

* Before contact with Europe, mourning wars were highly ritualized forms of conflict meant primarily to restore harmony and balance. The Wendat and Iroquois believed that families— and, by extension, lineages, bands, and villages—lost power when a son, father, mother, or daughter died.

* To restore power, surviving kin needed to "requicken the dead" through rituals of adoption and reincorporation; that is, a lost person needed to be replaced. This was a physical and literal replacement but also symbolic.

- Warfare, thus, was typically small scale. The objective of seizing captives was to take people alive. And casualties were to be avoided because losing too many of one's own defeated the purpose of restoring balance. In this sense, warfare was meant to be integrative, not destructive.

- In the context of mourning wars, the Wendat and Iroquois were attractive foes because of their commonalities. Their many similarities, in other words, held the promise of easier adoptions, although they still practiced ritual torture.

Beaver Wars

- By the 1640s, the mourning wars morphed into the Beaver Wars. In short, the people were transformed by population collapse, political chaos, dislocations, and increased competition over the control of resources. Although spiritual motivations for warfare persisted, we also see the increasing importance of economic and geopolitical motives.

- Trade introduced things that became attractive to Native people, and when we think of trade, inevitably, we think of guns. Thus, we see two needs intensifying for Native peoples in the early 17th century: the spiritual need to requicken the dead and the need to increase trade. Driven by these two needs, the Iroquois launched military campaigns against their neighbors: the Algonquin, the Innu, the Lenape, the Susquehannock, and the Catawba.

- By the mid-1630s, the Wendat, devastated by epidemics, sent emissaries to forge an alliance with the French to defend themselves from the Iroquois. At the same time, the Iroquois forged an alliance with the Dutch, resulting in their gaining a decisive firearms advantage. Soon thereafter, Iroquois war parties overran neighboring peoples in search of furs and captives.

- By the 1640s, the mourning wars, predicated on the idea of restoring balance, had given way to the Beaver Wars, which were about access to resources and control of trade. The promise of a measured separatism between the Wendat and Iroquois fell apart.

- The Wendat were blown out of their homelands. Some sought refuge in Quebec, along the St. Lawrence. Others moved into the interior, above Georgia Bay or Michilmackinac. Still more went to Pontchartrain at the northwest edge of Lake Erie and the Sundusky Valley. Many of the Neutral, Petun, and Erie survivors were incorporated into the Iroquois or the Wendat, contributing in some cases to the emergence of distinct nations, such as the Wyandot.

- During the 1680s and 1690s, the Beaver Wars resumed, bringing further dislocation to the Wendat, as well as Algonquian- and Siouan-speaking peoples in the Great Lakes region. By the late 17th century, the area comprised two distinct zones: a land filled with refugee communities along the west coast of Lake Michigan and "emptied lands" located between the southern edge of the Great Lakes and the Ohio River.

- Even as their lives were being transformed by forces unleashed by colonialism, Indian communities continued to transform those forces, as well. To withstand the Iroquois onslaught, these refugee communities forged complex and tenuous alliances with one another and with the French. In so doing, Native ideas regarding diplomacy persisted.

- By the end of the 17th century, combined Native and French forces delivered a series of defeats to the Iroquois and British, who had by then supplanted the Dutch.

- The peace that followed, however, merely represented the beginning of a new phase in the complex relations between Natives and newcomers, and these relations would prove to be no less tenuous or complicated. They would leave no one unchanged.

Suggested Reading

Fenton, *The Great Law and the Longhouse*.

Parmenter, *The Edge of the Woods*.

Richter, *The Ordeal of the Longhouse*.

Sioui, *Huron Wendat*.

Trigger, *The Children of Aataentsic*.

Questions to Consider

1. In what ways did Native people transform the English and French colonial projects, even as their lives were being transformed by them?

2. How does the case study of mourning wars reveal the unique ways in which the Iroquois and Wendat made sense of the destabilizing impacts of disease, trade, and imperial entanglement?

INDIAN-EUROPEAN ENCOUNTERS, 1700–1750

Lecture 6

During the 1720s, a headman from a tribal community in the Carolina Piedmont presented the governor of South Carolina with a map, depicting individual Native groups and lines connecting them to Charleston, South Carolina, and the colony of Virginia. This map suggests the need to readjust our vision to understand the late 17th and early 18th centuries from Native perspectives. It indicates that the idea that Europeans controlled much of anything was illusory. According to historian Kathleen DuVal, "Rather than being colonized, Indians drew a successive series of European empires into local patterns of land and resource allocation, sustenance, goods exchange, gender relations, diplomacy, and warfare." In this lecture, we'll explore this multifaceted process of incorporation.

The Covenant Chain

❖ The Senecas, Cayugas, Onondagas, Oneidas, and Mohawks served as the member nations of the Iroquois Confederacy, though they referred to themselves as the Haudenosaunee, or People of the Longhouse.

❖ How and why did the Iroquois become the People of the Longhouse, united in a great league of peace and power? We find the answer in a centuries-old oral history of the Confederacy's origins: the Deganawida Epic.

  › The epic tells of a time of great warfare. Amid this tumult, Hiawatha, who soon would become a leader of the nascent Iroquois Confederacy, lost his three daughters. Dictates of the mourning wars would've called him to seek out his enemies and requicken the dead by killing or adopting an enemy, thereby restoring his lineage, clan, and village. Another native leader, Deganawida—a Wendat who had been adopted by the Iroquois—came to see Hiawatha.

- > Known as the Peacemaker, Deganawida taught Hiawatha that there was a better way than seeking revenge through war: the rituals of condolence. Deganawida also taught him ritual means of bringing the Iroquois people into a union—to be called the League of the Iroquois or the Great League of Peace.
- > Within the Great League, each nation would retain control over its own local affairs. Through a Grand Council, they would meet, discuss, and make decisions about things of common concern. War would no longer be needed to settle disputes.
- > Together, the story continues, the Five Nations of the Iroquois Confederacy would observe the Great Law, and they would be as a bundle of arrows or a treaty of peace. They would supplant destructive and unsustainable wars with the Condolence Council.

❖ According to Lumbee legal scholar Robert Williams, the Iroquois viewed the Deganawida Epic as offering a paradigm for all international relations, including those with the European newcomers. Treaty making, then, became an extension of the Great League of Peace.

❖ The concept of a measured separatism was an integral component of treaty making, both among Native tribes and with colonial settlers. This can be seen in the Gushwenta—or Two-Row Wampum Belt—dating in the Iroquois tradition to a 1613 treaty with the Dutch. Running parallel to each other, the rows are emblematic of two nations that respect each other's sovereignty.

❖ After the English supplanted the Dutch in present-day New York during the 1660s, the Iroquois extended the relationship of mutuality, reciprocity, kinship, and measured separatism that was woven into the Two-Row Wampum Belt to them.

❖ The Iroquois called this alliance the Covenant Chain and likened it to a series of silver links that need to be "kept bright" at regular intervals through councils and treaties that dealt with everything from conflict to commerce.

- ❖ The Iroquois also used the Covenant Chain to engage in what European contemporaries called "modern Indian politics." And neither the French nor the British, the major European imperial powers in the Northeast by the late 18th century, liked it very much.

- ❖ That's because "modern Indian politics" was, in fact, a carefully constructed and managed playoff system. The Iroquois used this playoff system to destabilize the imperial aspirations of the Europeans, and to advance their own. In so doing, the Iroquois used diplomacy, trade, and alliance—that is, the Covenant Chain—to advance their own interests and to preserve their own independence.

The Lenape People

- ❖ Other Native peoples, including the Lenape, or Delaware, people, experienced very different relations with the various colonies along the Eastern Seaboard.

- ❖ At the time of contact with Europeans, the Lenape might have had a total population of 8,000 to 12,000. They saw themselves as related bands that lived in villages of a few hundred members

Chief of the Lenape

each. These village bands cooperated in times of crisis or seasonal hunting.

- By the early 18th century, the Delaware had concentrated in what is today Pennsylvania. There, William Penn and the Quakers generally earned a reputation of dealing fairly with tribal communities. Lands were obtained, more often than not, through negotiated treaties.

- But in 1737, the Lenape were the victims of one of the most infamous land grabs in American Indian history—the so-called Walking Purchase.
  - Thomas Penn—son of the colony's founder—claimed to have found a deed made in 1686, in which the Lenape granted his father land "as far as a man can go in a day and a half" and, from there, down the course of the Delaware River.
  - The Pennsylvanians produced a team of runners to walk out the deed, and they cleared a path for the runners in advance. In the end, the colonial relay team had covered about 65 miles and taken from the Lenape the last of their lands in the upper Delaware and Lehigh valleys.
  - The Lenape did not take this lying down, however. They complained to the Pennsylvania authorities—in no uncertain terms.

- To counter Lenape dissent, the Pennsylvanians turned to the Iroquois for support. In the summer of 1742—during a council in Philadelphia—the Onondaga leader Canasatego asserted Iroquois superiority over the Lenape and insisted that they accept their fate. Clearly, the Iroquois were taking advantage of the situation to shore up their own place in colonial politics at the expense of the Lenape.

- In turn, the Lenape set out on a long journey to the west that would take them into the Ohio Country just in time to be caught, once again, between the hammer and anvil of competing imperial and tribal powers.

Upper Ohio Country

- As a consequence of ongoing Iroquois attacks in the area during the late 17th century, we can think of the Ohio Country as comprising two zones.

- The first zone was located to the west of Lake Michigan and took the shape of an inverted triangle. This zone was filled with refugee peoples from the east and the north. Sometimes these were entire communities that had moved away in search of safety in the wake of Haudenosaunee expansion. But many of the Ohio Country's refugee communities were also a multiethnic polyglot that included the Wendat, Anishinaabeg, Odawa, Potawatomi, Myaamia, Shawnee, Sauk, and Fox.

- The second zone was located from the southern edges of the Great Lakes to the Ohio River and might be thought of as "emptied lands." These were the former homelands of tribes that had been blown out by the Iroquois during the invasion from the east over the course of the 17th century.

- "The middle ground" is Stanford historian Richard White's conception of a cultural, political, social, and economic phenomenon that rests "in between cultures, people, and in between empires and the nonstate world of villages." Was this what held the fragmented indigenous communities together?

- These communities shared a common space—many of them because they had forced from their own homelands into a new area. Because of that, they also frequently shared a common enemy: the Iroquois.

- But newly shared locations and experiences did not necessarily guarantee peace. Instead, Native people made peace and forged a sense of commonality. Thinking and speaking in terms of kinship, the tribal communities of the Upper Ohio Country built relationships of mutual obligation that were affirmed and renewed through gift giving, trade, intermarriage, and ritual.

- This did not, however, lead inevitably to a "pan-tribal" political alliance. The process of coordinating and mobilizing the alliances that Native people were forging in the Upper Ohio Country involved the presence of still another newcomer—a European one.
    - As conflict over the control of Ohio Country hunting grounds continued through the late 17th century, the French became central to an alliance with the Myaamia, Shawnee, and Potawatomi, and other tribal nations. Acting in concert, they were able to marshal enough power to invade Iroquoia, the Iroquois homeland, and score important victories there by the late 1690s.
    - This, in turn, led to a massive treaty council held in Montreal in 1701. Featuring the involvement of the French, the Iroquois, and tribes from the Ohio Country, the Grand Settlement of 1701 brought an end to the fighting.
    - Although the relative peace that followed the Grand Settlement might appear to have been a pinnacle for the French and Indian alliance, in fact, it contributed to the reassertion of more disparate and localized tribal identities that were not as closely tied to the French.
    - The Grand Settlement meant that such people as the Myaamia could reclaim ground they had lost to the Iroquois and new multitribal communities could form in the once-emptied lands of the Ohio Country. The increasing presence of English traders, who moved into this space from the east during the middle decades of the 18th century, suggested that the Grand Settlement had not actually settled matters at all.

- A different story emerges when we move into the Arkansas River Valley. This, according to historian Kathleen DuVal, would be considered more accurately as Native ground, rather than a middle ground.
    - In the Arkansas River Valley, the Osage and Quapaw were able to maintain their sovereignty and independence by drawing the Spanish and French into their worlds as they understood them. This included everything from land, resources, and trade to gender relations, diplomacy, and war.

> The tribes were so powerful that European imperial expansion really came to be a competition over Indian allies—the newcomers, in other words, had very little power of their own.

The Southeast

- In the Southeast, increased social and economic interactions with colonists made it increasingly difficult for Native people to control the rate and shape of change. Their search for common ground was challenged even more by the spread of diseases, the expansion of slavery, and the onset of war.

- Between 1711 and 1713, for instance, the Tuscarora people fought—and lost—a devastating war against the British and their Yamasee allies in North Carolina. Several hundred Tuscaroras were taken into slavery. The other survivors moved north, seeking refuge with the Haudenosaunee, with whom they shared the Iroquois language. Unable to preserve their Native ground in North Carolina, the Tuscarora joined the Iroquois Confederacy, becoming its sixth nation, in 1722.

- Meanwhile, the Yamasee in South Carolina experienced similar trauma that led to war in 1715. This was a complex conflict that involved several tribal nations, each with their own reasons for being involved. While it ended at various times for various parties, the war had largely come to an end by 1718. Although the Yamasee faced hardships, they, like the Tuscarora, became a part of other tribal groups, including the emerging Creek Confederacy and the Seminole.

- In the wake of this destructive war, refugees from fragmented tribal communities in South Carolina, such as the Cheraw, Waxhaw, and Wateree, coalesced to form a larger confederacy of peoples that would in time be referred to collectively as the Catawba.

❖ The story that defined the late 17th and early 18th centuries for much of Native America was one of how Native people engaged in a process of mutual incorporation and reciprocal transformation to preserve Native ground. But it remained to be seen how long the Native ground could last.

Suggested Reading

DuVal, *The Native Ground.*

Merrell, *Into the American Woods.*

Richter, *The Ordeal of the Longhouse.*

White, *The Middle Ground.*

Williams, *Linking Arms Together.*

Questions to Consider

1. What is the Deganawida Epic, and how is it related to the Covenant Chain that the Iroquois forged with Europeans? What does this tell us about how Native people approached the latest newcomers? In what ways do the Deganawida Epic, Covenant Chain, and treaties offer paradigms for behavior?

2. What is the phrase "Native Ground" meant to convey, and where do you see examples of it in this lecture? How do the stories presented in this lecture complicate the master narrative regarding the early colonial period?

Lecture 7

THE SEVEN YEARS' WAR IN INDIAN COUNTRY

What did the so-called French and Indian War, known alternatively as the Seven Years' War, mean to American Indians? For some people, it served as a victory; for others, it served as a defeat. And for a greater number still, it had no immediate impact. In this lecture, we won't think about the 1750s and 1760s as the period in which the British defeated the French and Indians, securing title to virtually all of North America east of the Mississippi River. Instead, we'll change the storyline by exploring the perspectives of Native people who experienced the era quite differently—tribal nations, largely in the Northeast and Ohio Country, that deployed both time-tested and innovative strategies to survive between European would-be empires.

Seven Years' War (1754–1763)

❖ By the mid-18th century, the British had established quite a colonial presence across the Eastern Seaboard and were pushing westward to the Appalachian Mountains. The French had built a vast trading network that began in the St. Lawrence River Valley and extended north of the Great Lakes, then down the Mississippi River to the Gulf of Mexico. The Ohio Country fit into the vast space between the Great Lakes and the Ohio River.

❖ Both the British and the French needed the Ohio River and the Ohio Country to sustain the economic foundations on which their dreams of extending their empires into North America rested. But even though both France and Great Britain claimed this territory, the Ohio Country remained Native ground, and everyone knew it. Europeans needed Indian allies to legitimate their claims to the land and to control the fur trade.

- The Native nations in the Ohio Country consisted of multiethnic tribal communities. Most of them were Algonquian speakers, but there were also Siouan and Iroquoian speakers. Many of these people were refugees living far away from their ancestral lands.

- There was a tendency among tribal communities to ally with the French—particularly moving from east to west within the Ohio Country. But the French recognized that force could not maintain the allegiance of indigenous nations. In testimony to Native power, the French adopted Native protocol in the context of diplomacy and exchange.

- By mid-century, the British were working hard to make inroads into the Ohio Country. This, in turn, prompted the French to establish Fort Duquesne, located at the intersection of the Ohio, Allegheny, and Monongahela Rivers. It served as the gateway into the Ohio Country and is where the French drew their line in the sand—which the British ignored.

- After a few skirmishes in the spring of 1754, a French-Algonquian force defeated a detachment of Virginia militia under the command of George Washington at Fort Necessity in July. Over the next 12 months, the French reinforced Fort Duquesne and shored up alliances with tribal nations. They needed both when British troops returned under the command of General Edward Braddock in July 1755.

- Braddock was unsuited for forging an alliance predicated largely on the idea of extending kinship ties with Indian people. In fact, according to historian Fred Anderson, he was downright insulting of their ability as warriors. But Braddock's army was decimated at Fort Duquesne by a largely Indian force. Braddock himself was among the casualties.

- By the time the French and English made formal declarations of war in 1756, the North American conflict had become global. Despite early French victories, the protracted war that followed turned in favor of the British and Iroquois. It proved devastating to the nations of the Ohio Country and, in the South, to the Cherokees.

- By 1758, the alliance that the Native people in the Ohio Country had forged with the French was faltering, largely because of the ravages of smallpox. The British also benefited from their ability to get their otherwise unruly colonies to cooperate with one another.

The Treaty of Paris

- In the fall of 1758, the Indians of the Ohio Country made peace with the British through the Treaty of Easton. Within a few months, the French withdrew from the forks of the Ohio, Allegheny, and Monongahela Rivers. For the French, the war was lost, though achieving peace took another five years.

- At the Treaty of Paris in 1763, the French surrendered all claims to lands between the Appalachian Mountains and the Mississippi River, as well as present-day Canada. Now, everything east of the Mississippi was claimed by the British, and everything west of the Mississippi was claimed by the Spanish. The problem was that there were no Indians at the table during the Treaty of Paris.

- Seen from Indian perspectives, the Seven Years' War resolved nothing. It may have pitted the French and Native peoples of the Ohio Country against the British and their Iroquois allies, but the indigenous peoples of the Ohio Country did not share French aims. They weren't fighting to legitimate French claims but to preserve their own lands.

- The Indians of the Ohio Country did not accept the idea that France could relinquish their claims to the British because it was not their land to cede. In fact, the only thing the French reasonably could have conveyed to the English in 1763, under the dictates of European law, would have been the right of first purchase. But the Indians weren't selling.

- Nonetheless, the French withdrawal from North America did not bode well for Indians in the Ohio Country. A forbidding symbol of British intentions came in the form of a bolstered (and now renamed) Fort Pitt, at the confluence of the Allegheny and Monongahela Rivers.

Pontiac's War (May 1763–July 1766)

- According to historian Gregory Evans Dowd, Pontiac's War was about the status of Native nations. The Indians of the Ohio Country, as we've seen, did not see themselves as subjects, and they liked it even less when they were treated that way by the British. We should view this pivotal event as a war for continued independence.

- Dowd also argues that the conflict was a "war under heaven," meaning that Native religious beliefs played a central role in the conflict. Native people, for instance, talked about their rights to the land being founded on the fact that they had been created in and for a particular place. Moreover, Native actions were informed by prophetic visions calling on Native people to restore power through right behavior and ritual activity, thereby ridding themselves of their dependency on Europeans.

- Pontiac was an Odawa born in the 1720s and raised in the area west of Lake Erie, near where the French founded Fort Detroit. Pontiac was a civil leader—or "most respected man"—who headed a network of extended families. Much of his authority came from his judgment and generosity. He may also have been a seeker of spiritual power, someone who was able to converse with spirits to transform and regenerate the world.

- In what way was a conflict associated so powerfully with Pontiac informed by religious beliefs? The answer lies in the way in which many Native people in the Ohio Country made sense of their loss of power and what it would take to restore it.

- For instance, we know that Native people were becoming increasingly dependent on British traders because of overhunting and the disappearance of game in the Ohio Country. We also know that Indians were forced to pay high prices for goods, which fostered indebtedness. Added to that was the constant encroachment by colonists and the presence of British soldiers, as they occupied abandoned French forts.

- British officials bruised Native feelings and perspectives by prohibiting gift giving and ritualized acts of reciprocity. Given their victory over the

French and their Indian allies, the British had no intentions of abiding by kinship expectations. Rather, they saw their dominion as something to be governed, not something to be negotiated. Treating Native people

Pontiac takes up the war hatchet

as though they were conquered subjects cut against Native people's own sense of themselves and their relationship with the British.

- In the spring of 1763, Pontiac and a vast intertribal alliance set out to restore their world to its former state. At Fort Detroit, Pontiac urged the Odawa, Potawatomi, and Ojibwe to accept Lenape war belts. Fashioned from black beads, they represented a call to arms to rid the Ohio Country of the British. Soon, they would be joined by the Myaamia, Wyandot, Kickapoo, Piankashaw, Shawnee, and others.

- Attacks on 13 British posts throughout the Upper Ohio Country followed. The combined Native forces rolled over the British forts of Miami, Sandusky, and St. Joseph, among others. In the spring of 1763, Native attacks on the pivotal strongholds of Fort Pitt, Fort Detroit, and Fort Niagara had turned into long-term sieges. Early on, however, British leaders ordered the dissemination of smallpox-infected blankets to a group of Lenape that had come to negotiate. The effects were devastating.

- Despite the ravages of biological warfare, the success of the indigenous military campaign in the Ohio Country forced the British government to respond to Native demands. In October 1763, King George III issued the Royal Proclamation, establishing a line that made the Appalachian Mountains the boundary between Indians and colonists. It also forbade private purchases of Indian land, restricted commerce to licensed traders, and ordered colonists west of the line to return to the east.

- However, the British did not agree to abandon their forts, and conflict erupted once more throughout the borderlands. The combined effects of British offensives in 1764, intertribal disputes, disease, and the absence of a European ally ultimately broke pan-Indian unity. By the summer of 1766, the conflict wound down. Pontiac made peace with the British, but in so doing, he fell out of standing with those in the intertribal alliance who wanted to continue the war.

Outcomes of the Wars

❖ The Seven Years' War and Pontiac's War were setbacks, but there were victories to be found within them. Although they may have lost their French ally, the Indians in the Ohio Country had managed to secure British recognition that they were not subjects but sovereign nations. What's more, the British begrudgingly restored their observance of indigenous diplomatic protocols.

❖ Most important of all—as the line drawn by the Royal Proclamation attested—the Indians of the Ohio Country had survived despite being caught between empires. They remained in possession of the land the Master of Life had created for them.

Suggested Reading

Anderson, *Crucible of War*.

Calloway, *The Scratch of a Pen*.

Dowd, *War Under Heaven*.

Jennings, *Empire of Fortune*.

Sleeper-Smith, *Indian Women and French Men*.

Questions to Consider

1. How did Native people try to make sense of finding themselves between empires?
2. How does the case study of Pontiac challenge the prevailing interpretation of the Seven Years' War as an event? Why does it make sense to refer to what happened after 1763 as a "war under heaven?"

THE AMERICAN REVOLUTION THROUGH NATIVE EYES

Lecture 8

Few events in U.S. history are more mythologized than the American Revolution. It evokes images of freedom-loving patriots and tyrannical monarchs. Yet we often forget that there are other perspectives on the American Revolution. In this lecture, we'll look at how Native people experienced the war in at least three different ways: as allies, as participants in their own civil wars, and as neutral parties.

The American Revolution as an "Event"

- For most American Indians east of the Mississippi River, the American Revolution represented one more in a long series of European wars for empire. West of the Mississippi River, the American Revolution wasn't even eventful—at least, not immediately so.

- Most Native peoples east of the Mississippi, having already been caught between imperial contests, initially sought neutrality in what one Oneida called an "unnatural" quarrel between "two brothers of one blood."

- American Indians surmised that these unnatural quarrels were intended ultimately to waste Native peoples and allow the whites to divide the land among themselves. From many Native perspectives, the Revolution simply represented a war between a British "father" and his land-hungry "children."

- What's more, it was the so-called patriots who were most responsible for the encroaching, exploiting, and killing. That was certainly the lesson Native people learned through the warfare that was endemic east of the Mississippi River during the 18th century.

- Taking the opposite view, it was the so-called tyrannical British monarchy who had drawn and sought to uphold the Proclamation Line of 1763—which tried to limit colonial expansion to the area east of the Appalachian Mountains—and who had to renegotiate that line in 1768, moving the boundary westward from the Appalachian Mountains to the Ohio River.

- From the perspective of many Native people, there would be no liberty for them under the rule of the colonists or the crown—not from colonists who appeared incapable of looking on them as human beings and not from a king who preferred to look at tribes as subjects rather than sovereign nations. Native people were in the position of having to make unenviable decisions: to ally with the colonists or the crown or to seek neutrality.

The Catawba

- At the time of the Revolution, the Catawba were located in the Piedmont, which stretches through the Carolinas. They were a diverse group of about 15 separate peoples, who identified themselves primarily according to the villages where they lived.

- These groups remade their identities in the wake of disease, war, enslavement, and dependency on trade as they coalesced. But the smallpox epidemics that followed in the wake of the Seven Years' War further weakened them. Thus, by the time of the American Revolution, the Catawba were in a difficult spot.

- Surrounded by hostile South Carolinians, they turned to renting their reservation land as a means of economic survival. Indeed, they had rented almost all of it by the 1770s, and only a small reservation remained. Once set apart, their villages had become surrounded by and interwoven with colonial communities.

- Ironically, in South Carolina the precarious peace based on fear of the powerful Catawba nation was replaced by more congenial relationships, even friendships—if unequal—as Catawba power faded. Thus, when the Revolutionary War erupted, the Catawba became patriots.

- Catawbas served with colonial forces against the British throughout the region. They also provided food and aid to colonists after the British captured Charleston, South Carolina, in May 1780. And when the colonial army fled the region and sought refuge on their reservation, the reservation became the center of ongoing resistance to the crown. But when the British advanced, the Catawba were forced to flee.

- After the war, part of the Catawba strategy to carve out their own niche in the new nation was to promote their patriotic service and sacrifice to the revolutionaries.

The Cherokee

- Further to the South, the Cherokee offer a different perspective. For them, it made sense to ally with the monarchy.

- For decades leading up to the Revolution, the Cherokee had found themselves in increasingly dire straits. During the 1730s and 1750s, smallpox took its toll. And the Seven Years' War, in which the Cherokees fought on the side of the British, brought hardship and significant land loss.

- By the time the American Revolution began, tensions within the Cherokee community were high. Younger, more militant leaders, including a Cherokee war chief named Dragging Canoe, pressed for military action rather than diplomatic accommodation. Backed by promises of British support, Dragging Canoe attempted to push out the colonists who had invaded Cherokee homelands and hunting grounds. He was allied with the Shawnee, Lenape, Mohawk, and others from the north and west.

- But the American Revolution brought disaster rather than independence to the Cherokee. Colonial forces destroyed Cherokee towns and cornfields, opening the door for accommodationists.

- In a series of treaties in the late 1770s and early 1780s, the Cherokee ceded even more land—about 5 million acres of it. When all was said and done, the American Revolution cost the Cherokee about 10,000 lives, 75 percent of their territory, and more than half of their towns. The fight, however, was far from over.

- Indeed, the faction that followed Dragging Canoe refused to recognize the treaties or the legitimacy of the accommodationist leaders. Instead, they formed a new community, the Chickamauga Cherokee, in Tennessee and northern Alabama. And from there, they continued to defend their homelands from the new nation of freedom-loving patriots into the 1790s. To these Cherokees, the American Revolution represented the opening of several more decades of hostilities that would end in forced removal.

Iroquoia

- All through the Seven Years' War, the Iroquois Confederacy had played the colonial powers off one another to retain their land, livelihood, and sovereignty. Tensions often ran high, but the Confederacy always seemed to hold. Yet rival appeals by the British and the colonists for their favor divided the Iroquois.

- The Seneca chief known as Cornplanter counseled neutrality. After initially following suit, the Oneida and Tuscarora advocated for an alliance with the revolutionaries. Meanwhile, Joseph Brant, a Mohawk, and Red Jacket, a Seneca, became the most ardent supporters of aiding the British. The Cayuga and Onondaga joined them.

- In 1777, the Iroquois decided to ritually extinguish the Council Fire at Onondaga. For the duration of the war, the Six Nations would not meet in council to make decisions. The American Revolution—as an event—was a civil war in Iroquoia that broke a peace among the nations that had existed for several hundred years.

- Iroquois land became a battleground once more. In 1779, for instance, Major General John Sullivan launched a campaign of terror against Britain's Iroquois allies that earned his commanding officer, George Washington, the name Town Destroyer in Seneca.

- In this war, however, Iroquoia was also a battleground that saw British-allied Mohawks and Senecas and American-allied Tuscaroras and Oneidas killing each other, as at the Battle of Oriskany in 1777. In the end, the pro-British faction of the Confederacy fled to Canada.

Gnadenhutten

- Gnadenhutten, on the edge of the Ohio Country, was a settlement founded by Moravian missionaries in 1772. When the Revolutionary War broke out a few years later, it served as the home of Lenape and Shawnee converts to Christianity. From here, we can see the perils of neutrality and the limits of accommodation.

- Having been pushed out of their ancestral homes in present-day New Jersey and eastern Pennsylvania during the 17th and 18th centuries, most of the Lenape had, by the 1770s, relocated around Fort Pitt, in the northern Ohio River Valley.

- The Lenape were divided among three factions: Some supported the British; others supported the colonists; and still another group wanted to remain neutral. Among the neutrals were Lenape who had joined the Shawnee at the Moravian settlements of Gnadenhutten, Salem, and Schoenbrunn, along the Tuscarawas River in eastern Ohio. These were agricultural missions that promoted assimilation. The residents also embraced Christianity and pacifism.

- The war put the Lenape and Shawnee in a difficult spot. Those who chose to go to war looked at the residents of Gnadenhutten, Salem, and Schoenbrunn with distrust. But the colonists viewed them similarly, fearing that they were aiding and abetting the Indians who were carrying out raids along borderland settlements in Pennsylvania and Virginia.

- In March 1782, as war spread across the borders, Pennsylvania set its sights on the Christian Indians at Gnadenhutten and Salem. A 100-person detachment of militia set out to deliver a killing blow under the pretense that the residents were either supporting Indian raids or taking part in them.

- Militiamen bludgeoned to death the Lenape and Shawnee Christians who resided there. The deceased numbered 29 men, 27 women, and 34 children. They also looted the town and burned it to the ground. When they returned to Fort Pitt, they murdered several more Lenapes who had sought refuge there. Colonel David Williamson—the leader of the killing—was considered a local hero.

- In June 1782, three months after the slaughter at Gnadenhutten, a larger assault was launched. About 488 colonial volunteers were sent to annihilate the Wyandot and Lenape in northern Ohio. Colonel Williamson was there, as were many of the militiamen who had been involved in the slaughter at Gnadenhutten.

- On June 4 and June 5, 1782, however, they met a combined Indian and British force on the plains of the upper Sandusky River. This time, the Americans were routed, with more than 70 killed in battle.

- Colonel William Crawford, the commander of the attack, was captured. With his body, the Wyandot Half-King and the Lenape Captain Pipe renewed the ritual torture of victims—to vindicate the victims of Gnadenhutten.

- For many Lenape, the American Revolution signified that neutrality was not an option. It signified that accommodation inevitably led to destruction. The 1778 Treaty of Fort Pitt had established a peace that brought no peace.

The American Revolution as a "Nonevent"

- By comparison, if we look west across the Mississippi, the American Revolution was virtually a nonevent during the 1770s and 1780s.

- In 1783, the Treaty of Paris brought an end to the war between the British and the Americans. The British yielded to the United States all land east of the Mississippi River and south of what would become the Canadian border.

- But as with the Treaty with the Lenape in 1778, it would be a peace that brought no peace to Indian Country. And as with the Treaty of Paris of 1763, the one in 1783 did not include any Native representation. Perhaps unsurprisingly, there was no recognition that much of the land being ceded was still Native ground.

- Looking at the American Revolution from the perspective of Native America, we can see it as an unnatural quarrel between brothers of the same blood, a catalyst for a civil war that caused deep divisions within Indian communities, a moment that involved perilous attempts to preserve neutrality, and an opportunity to make the choice—unenviable as it was—to ally with one's enemies.

❖ Taken together, the 1770s and 1780s are best understood as a moment that compelled tribes in the east to make hard choices and develop strategies to pursue their interests. In succeeding decades, Native people would call on these strategies and others as the new United States proclaimed its intention to realize one people's freedom through another's dispossession by way of policy it called "expansion with honor."

Suggested Reading

Calloway, *The American Revolution in Indian Country*.

DuVal, *Independence Lost*.

Merrell, *The Indians' New World*.

Saunt, *West of the Revolution*.

White, *The Middle Ground*.

Questions to Consider

1. How did the Abenaki, Catawba, Lenape, Iroquois, and Cherokee experience the American Revolution? How do those experiences challenge the prevailing narrative about it?

2. What happened to the peoples who sought to ally with, or at least accommodate the presence of, the revolutionary colonists? How did these outcomes reflect on the latter's vision of freedom, liberty, and fraternity?

Lecture 9: INDIAN RESISTANCE IN THE OHIO COUNTRY

In this lecture, we'll explore how the Treaty of Paris of 1783—which settled the American Revolutionary War between England and the colonists—might have brought an end to the unnatural quarrel between "two brothers of one blood," but it brought no peace to Native peoples. Instead, it served as a catalyst for resistance and revitalization movements in Iroquoia, across the Ohio Country, and into the Southeast from the 1790s through the early 19th century. To tell that story, we'll look at a pan-tribal alliance that secured military victories during the 1790s and the rise of the Shawnee brothers Tenskwatawa and Tecumseh, who spearheaded a very different kind of resistance movement two decades later.

"Expansion with Honor"

- In the wake of the American Revolution, the future of the United States was uncertain. Moreover, the British to the north and the Spanish to the south made for unfriendly neighbors. These realities shaped the policies that the United States adopted toward indigenous nations.

- The new nation's zeal to expand by taking Indian land gave rise to a document called the Northwest Ordinance. Adopted in 1787, it established a mechanism for governing territories and a process for admitting them into the Union as states. The intent of the Northwest Ordinance was the orderly assimilation of land formerly claimed by the British. Congress called it the Northwest Territory, but it was the Ohio Country, and it was still very much Native ground.

- According to the Northwest Ordinance, "The utmost good faith shall always be observed towards the Indians." The principle of "utmost good faith" informed the entire Indian policy crafted by Secretary of War Henry Knox. Knox called it "expansion with honor," at the heart of which was the continuation of the British policy of treaty making, or the forging of nation-to-nation agreements.

- The problem was that the United States, like Britain, tended to think of treaties as expedient tools, rather than as long-standing covenants. They were vehicles for the United States to clear title to Indian land.

- Yet the new and still-weak U.S. federal government was unable to prevent individual states—or citizens, for that matter—from negotiating ad hoc agreements. Nor could it stop settlers from squatting on Indian land or traders from taking advantage of Native people.

Native Nations of the Ohio Country

- During the 1790s, the Native nations of the Ohio Country had no intention of yielding their sovereign claims. They held the Ohio River to be an inviolable border and could point to its recognition in the Treaty of Fort Stanwix in 1768, the Treaty of Paris in 1783, and a second Treaty of Fort Stanwix in 1784.

- As Native people faced pressure to cede land through what is today New York, Pennsylvania, Ohio, Kentucky, and Indiana, a confederacy of Iroquois, Wyandot, Lenape, Shawnee, Odawa, Ojibwe, Cherokee, Myaamia, and others nations attempted to hold the line.

- In November and December 1786, delegates from this confederacy sent a message to Congress in which they affirmed the Ohio River as the dividing line and rejected the piecemeal treaties that had been signed in the past. Only treaties that enjoyed the unanimous support of all the tribal nations would be considered valid.

- The United States ignored this appeal and attempted to flex its muscle. The results were catastrophic—for the United States. In October 1790, and again in November 1791, the northwestern Indian confederacy crushed American invasion forces under the command of Generals Josiah Harmar and Arthur St. Clair.

- But military resistance—and winning, at that—was not the only way that Native people in the Ohio Country were conducting their lives. An old buffalo wallow in the north-central part of the Ohio Country was the headquarters of the resistance movement.
    - Known as the Glaize, it was also the residence of about 2,000 Shawnee, Lenape, and Myaamia. The Glaize was constituted of refugees from conflicts throughout the Ohio Country during the 1790s, as well as people of French, British, and African ancestry.
    - In 1793, the Glaize became the target for yet another American assault. General Anthony Wayne, commanding an estimated force of 3,000 well-equipped soldiers, set out from Fort Washington in Cincinnati, marching north toward the Glaize. The tribal nations were able to muster perhaps 1,300 warriors to meet them.
    - On August 20, Wayne's army engaged the confederated Indian force on the west bank of the Maumee River. In the wake of the Battle of Fallen Timbers, the largely Algonquian force retreated toward Fort Miami, a nearby fortification still occupied by the British.
    - The Indians of the Ohio Country held the hope that the British might become their "father" once more. But at Fort Miami, the British refused them sanctuary.

- Defeat at the Battle of Fallen Timbers proved disastrous. The British refusal of aid and Wayne's destruction of the Natives' food supply forced the intertribal confederation to the treaty table.

- In August 1795, after eight months of negotiations, the Treaty of Greenville ceded land that included two-thirds of present-day Ohio, portions of Indiana and Michigan, and strategic locations in Illinois. The treaty ended a remarkable period of pan-tribal cooperation, inaugurated the "civilization program" in the Ohio Country, and opened the Ohio River Valley to a flood of settlers. In so doing, it virtually guaranteed that the new "permanent boundaries" between Indians and whites in the northwest corner of Ohio would not last.

Tecumseh and Tenskwatawa

- The two most instrumental figures in the next wave of resistance were the Shawnee brothers Tecumseh and Tenskwatawa (known as the Shawnee Prophet).

  - One of the ways in which Tecumseh and Tenskwatawa built a pan-tribal alliance in the wake of the Treaty of Greenville was to encourage Shawnee, Miami, Ojibwe, Odawa, and other people to see themselves as sharing a common identity as Indians. Tecumseh and Tenskwatawa also rooted their movement for pan-tribal unity in the land.

  Tecumseh

  - Tenskwatawa, after receiving a vision in the spring of 1805, called for emissaries from other tribal communities to adopt the new rituals he taught as a means to restore balance, harmony, and power.

- Often, the focal points of conflict were the federal government's civilization program and the chiefs who were its leading proponents. Some leaders embraced the government's emphasis on training Indians to become self-sufficient. Others believed that the program fostered dependency on outsiders through trade and annuities. It introduced alien concepts about ownership and wealth that caused Native people to be jealous and covetous of one another. It also gave Christian missionaries too much power.

- In the spring of 1806, the Shawnee brothers made a provocative move by relocating their village across the line established by the Treaty of Greenville. The following year, it began to look as if the old alliance with Great Britain might be realized once again.

- In response, future U.S. President William Henry Harrison—then Indiana's territorial governor and a veteran of the Battle of Fallen Timbers—overtly challenged the legitimacy of Tenskwatawa's prophetic vision and Tecumseh's political authority.

- Federal efforts to secure land cessions continued at the same time. The governors of the Indiana and Michigan territories secured six treaties between 1804 and 1809 that chipped away still more Native land in Michigan, Indiana, Illinois, and Ohio.

- As a consequence, the resistance movement grew stronger. Tenskwatawa established another new village, called Prophetstown, along the Wabash River, on lands belonging to the Myaamia.

- Harrison resolved to drive them out and pave the way, once and for all, for Indiana statehood. His efforts led to the Treaty of Fort Wayne in 1809. There, the United States secured a cession of 2.5 million acres, including the land on which Prophetstown had been established.

- As white settlers invaded the Northwest Territory, Tecumseh demanded that no land be sold without the consent of all Indians. Only this could break the hold of the "annuity chiefs" who, from his point of view, were destroying tribal sovereignty.

- In an attempt to rally the confederacy that had proved so successful during the early 1790s, Tecumseh dispatched emissaries to bring even more allies into the fold. By 1810, Shawnee diplomacy brought rewards, Prophetstown grew, and the alliance strengthened. In response, Harrison reinforced his headquarters at Vincennes, Indiana.

- In August 1810, Tecumseh and Harrison met as equals in a negotiation that set them on a course for war. The main topic of conversation was the Treaty of Fort Wayne. Tecumseh argued that the few signatories of the treaty had no right to cede Indian land that belonged to the many. Harrison coldly rejected everything he said, and neither gave ground.

- In November 1811, Harrison approached Prophetstown with an army of 1,000 strong. After an initial meeting with the Americans, Tenskwatawa met in council and persuaded his people to launch a preemptive strike.

- In the early hours of November 7, a combined force of Kickapoo, Ho-Chunk, Shawnee, and Potawatomi initiated the assault. Harrison had prepared for it and emerged the victor, despite suffering more casualties. Prophetstown itself was destroyed in the debacle a few days later.

- This defeat served as the beginning, rather than the end, of fighting. Tecumseh, on his return from the South, scolded Tenskwatawa. But the confederacy had held. And by June 1812, about 4,000 warriors were part of the alliance.

- At this point, the War of 1812 intersected with the resistance movement in the Ohio Country. The British, in desperate need of Indian allies to renew their campaign against the United States, agreed to help Tecumseh restore the Ohio River as the boundary line, should they emerge victorious.

- The British-Indian alliance subsequently routed American forces six times larger than their own south of Fort Detroit. Together, Tecumseh and British officer Isaac Brock masterminded the taking of Fort Detroit without as much as a shot.

- However, Brock was killed at the Battle of Queenston Heights in October 1812. The commitment of his successor, Henry Procter, to the Ohio Country was not strong. After a year of ineffective engagements, Proctor withdrew to Niagara. Tecumseh felt betrayed, and in a speech in September 1813, he steeled the resolve of the Native contingent to carry on.

- The high-water mark of the fighting came in October 1813, at the Battle of the Thames, or Moraviantown, in Ontario. There, the British-Indian alliance suffered a major defeat after withdrawing from Michigan and being intercepted by a pursuing American force. In the face of an attack orchestrated by Harrison, Tecumseh and his Indian warriors were the only ones to fight.

- Badly outnumbered and outgunned, the British retreated. Tecumseh and the Indians fought on but to no avail. Tecumseh took a bullet to the chest and was killed.

- In the Ohio Country, Tenskwatawa attempted to adjust to the world that "expansion with honor" had created. In 1826, he relocated with several hundred other Shawnees to a village in Kansas, where he died, alienated from his people and largely forgotten by non-Indians. By the time of his passing in 1836, many non–Native Americans became convinced that there was no place for Native people anywhere east of the Mississippi River.

Suggested Reading

Dowd, *A Spirited Resistance.*

Edmunds, *The Shawnee Prophet.*

Martin, *Sacred Revolt.*

Tanner, "The Glaize of 1792."

White, *The Middle Ground.*

Questions to Consider

1. What is "expansion with honor," and what was virtuous and contradictory about it?

2. How did Tecumseh and Tenskwatawa propose to restore sacred power? Was theirs a backward-looking vision that called for a return to tradition, or something else?

INDIAN REMOVAL: MANY TRAILS, MANY TEARS

Lecture 10

Between June 1838 and March 1839, the U.S. government forcibly removed the Cherokee from their homelands in Georgia, North Carolina, Alabama, and Tennessee to the Indian Territory—an area in the northeastern region of present-day Oklahoma. In an event known to the Cherokee as "The Trail Where They Cried," an estimated 16,000 refugees made the exodus; at least one-quarter died in the camps or perished along the way. The Trail of Tears is, without question, one of the most dramatic events in American Indian history. In this lecture, we'll explore the story behind it.

Origins of the Removal Crisis

❖ After the American Revolution, British defeat paved the way for a series of land cessions that resulted in the loss of 20,000 square miles of Cherokee land, including rich and vital hunting grounds. Yet the Cherokee found a surprising ally in the U.S. government against the almost immediate invasion of their lands by Georgians and North Carolinians.

❖ During the 1780s and 1790s, the Cherokee signed treaties with the United States to deflect the threats posed by these and other states. The treaties may have involved land cessions, but they also acknowledged Cherokee territorial boundaries. In addition, the Cherokee accepted the U.S. offer to extend its "civilization program" to them. Both treaty making and this civilization program were integral parts of the U.S. Indian policy known as "expansion with honor." But, in time, they would also become integral parts of the Cherokee policy of resisting it.

❖ As president between 1801 and 1809, Thomas Jefferson adopted policies that did not bode well for the Cherokee. For instance, he continued the civilization program, but he also revealed an ulterior motive by advocating for the use of trade as a means of fostering dependency, reasoning that it would more swiftly force tribal nations to the treaty table.

- Even more ominously for Native peoples, the Jefferson administration oversaw the Louisiana Purchase in 1803, a move that added more than 800,000 square miles to the territory claimed by the United States. This ignited fueled demands for expansion, which, in turn, contributed to brutal violence, land cessions, and war that brought an end to effective Indian military resistance in the Ohio Country and the Southeast between 1790 and 1815.

- Native communities in the East were quickly becoming surrounded and perceived as anachronistic. More non-Native voices, including those of state and territorial governors, the press, and pundits, demanded that the federal government forcibly remove tribes throughout the Southeast and Great Lakes region to areas west of the Mississippi River.

Struggle in Georgia

- By the 1820s, Georgia's political leaders argued that the state had already waited too long for removal, pointing to an agreement it had forged with Jefferson's administration in 1802 called the Georgia Compact.

- In keeping with this agreement, the federal government paid Georgia $1.2 million to relinquish its claims to lands in present-day Alabama and Mississippi. In return, President Jefferson agreed to use federal treaty power to extinguish tribal land claims within the state's limits "peaceably and on reasonable terms."

- After more than two decades of federal inaction—and, no less important, the discovery of gold in north Georgia—the state took matters into its own hands. In 1828, Georgia passed a law stating its intention to extend civil and criminal jurisdiction over the Cherokee in 1830—a move that would surely diminish if not completely destroy Cherokee sovereignty.

- The state bolstered its argument by pointing to a Supreme Court ruling in the case *Johnson v. M'Intosh* of 1823. This decision reasoned that the "doctrine of discovery" invested absolute underlying title in the "discovering nation" (in this case, the United States) to the lands being discovered (in this case, Indian land). In other words, being "discovered" meant that indigenous people immediately became mere tenants with nothing more than occupancy rights to lands they had lived in for thousands of years.

- The plot thickened when Georgia unexpectedly argued that it had inherited title to Indian lands within its boundaries when it declared independence from the British, the original discovering nation. This happened before the founding of the United States, and the state did not relinquish its claim to title afterward.

- Cherokee leaders well understood the origins of the removal crisis and discerned what consequences it carried for their people and homelands. The leaders met the crisis by engaging in a nation-building campaign and then, in classic American fashion, by taking Georgia to court. They used strategic accommodation to reinforce their separate nationality, resist removal, and preserve their aboriginal lands. Among other approaches, nation building also expressed itself in political change. In 1818, the Cherokee established the Cherokee Republic.

- Between July 4 and 26, 1827, the Cherokee convened to adopt a new constitution, defining a system of government that featured a bicameral legislature, an executive branch, and a judiciary. No less important, it clearly delineated territorial boundaries and reaffirmed the "common ownership" of the land. Two years later, the National Council made the selling of tribal lands without its approval punishable by death and established a national police force to ensure law and order.

- The conflict between Georgia and the Cherokee Nation reached a crossroad in 1828. That year, a national presidential election brought to power Andrew Jackson, known as an Indian fighter and a proponent of removal. Jackson was also seen as a champion of the common man, meaning that he would open new lands—Indian lands—for white settlement.

- As president, Jackson couched his support for forced removal in altruistic terms, suggesting that the Indian Territory would afford Indians "protection" from unscrupulous whites. Living in "peace and solitude" would further enable tribes to abandon their "wandering state" and embrace "civilization."

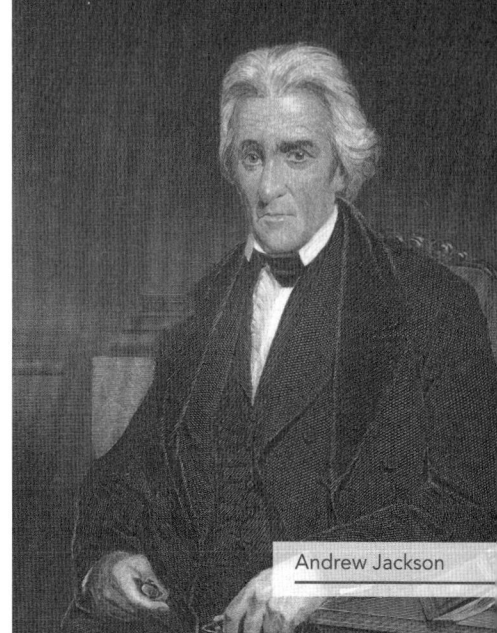
Andrew Jackson

- In the midst of rising tensions in Georgia and after bitter debate, Congress enacted legislation that changed the dynamics of the crisis. The Indian Removal Act of 1830 gave congressional sanction to complete the removal of tribes residing east of the Mississippi River.

- Led by Principal Chief John Ross and National Council member Major Ridge, the Cherokee placed their faith in the rule of law and opted to fight back by taking Georgia to court. The effort led to a pair of landmark Supreme Court decisions, *Cherokee Nation v. Georgia* in 1831 and *Worcester v. Georgia* in 1832. These decisions and the 1823 case *Johnson v. M'Intosh* form what is known as the Marshall Trilogy.

- In the first case, Ross challenged Georgia's right to exercise jurisdiction over the Cherokee Nation. But Chief Justice John Marshall argued that the Supreme Court would not hear the matter because the Cherokee Nation was not a "foreign state." He explained that tribal nations should be defined as "domestic dependent nations."

- The second case, *Worcester v. Georgia*, was made possible by a Georgia law that made it illegal for non-Indians to reside within the Cherokee Nation without first taking an oath of allegiance to the state. Missionaries Samuel Worcester and Elizur Butler refused to take the oath or leave the Cherokee Nation. By challenging Georgia's right to arrest, try, and sentence them, the missionaries provided an admissible way for the Supreme Court to hear the question of tribal versus state sovereignty.
  › In the case, the court ruled that the state did not have the right to arrest the Indian missionaries, and by extension, it declared unconstitutional all the laws that the state had passed over the Cherokee Nation.
  › In so doing, *Worcester* affirmed a federal system that included three distinct sovereign entities. By order of authority, they were federal, tribal, and state. Although tribes had been denominated "domestic dependent nations," Marshall reasoned, they still retained all the attributes of sovereignty that they did not voluntarily surrender to the federal government.
  › The chief justice also limited his original definition of the discovery doctrine. When discovering nations gained underlying title to aboriginal lands, he clarified, it granted an exclusive right to first purchase, and the right of first purchase belonged to the federal government.
  › This is what led him to reject Georgia's argument. The state could not "inherit" title to Cherokee lands, and because of that, neither could it violate Cherokee sovereignty through the extension of state jurisdiction.

Forced Exodus

- Bolstered by President Jackson's indifference, Georgia moved forward with a land lottery it originally authorized in 1830 that distributed Cherokee lands to non-Indians without the Cherokee Nation's consent. As settlers flooded in and pressure mounted, Cherokees split into pro- and anti-removal factions.

- On one side was Major Ridge; his son, John; and *Cherokee Phoenix* editor Elias Boudinot, who led a small group of Cherokees known as the

Treaty Party. They advocated for a negotiated exchange of lands that would require removal but preserve Cherokee sovereignty. They were opposed by John Ross and the vast majority of Cherokees, who refused to abandon their ancestral homelands.

- In December 1835, three years after the *Worcester* decision, the pro-removal faction—without the consent of the National Council and knowing that it could mean their lives—negotiated the Treaty of New Echota. Ross responded by demanding that the U.S. Senate refuse to ratify the treaty but to no avail. In the spring of 1836, it gained the force of law.

- Through the treaty, the Cherokee relinquished their claims to lands in the east in exchange for a new homeland in present-day northeastern Oklahoma. In addition, they received $5 million, as well as the promise of transportation to the west and assistance from the U.S. government for one year after removal. They were given two years to prepare.

The Trail of Tears

- The Cherokee were unprepared for what came in the spring of 1838. In May, soldiers arrived and drove Cherokees in Georgia, Tennessee, Alabama, and North Carolina to stockades, where untold numbers died. In June, a small detachment departed for the West, only to suffer tremendously in the hot, dry summer.

- In response to the overwhelming hardship and tragedy, Ross belatedly convinced the federal government to allow the Cherokee to oversee the rest of the removal. The results were no better for the 13 detachments leaving between August and December 1838 and arriving between January and late March 1839. All told, between 4,000 and 8,000 Cherokees lost their lives during the ordeal, including Ross's wife, Quatie.

- The Cherokee Nation seemed shattered beyond repair, and they were not the only people to experience the trauma of removal. Thirty-eight federally recognized tribes survive in Oklahoma, and all of them share one thing in common: an exodus from their ancestral homelands.

❖ A civil war erupted within the Cherokee Nation and did not end until 1846. Only then, nearly 10 years after their exodus, could Cherokees truly begin the arduous task of rebuilding their nation—a nation that, against all odds, endured.

❖ More than 150 years after her people's forced removal, Cherokee Principal Chief Wilma Mankiller offered a poignant reminder of the terrible costs of Cherokee survival: "Although it is so crucial for us to focus on the good things—our tenacity, our language and culture, the revitalization of tribal communities," Mankiller observed, "it is also important that we never forget what happened to our people on the Trail of Tears. It was indeed our holocaust."

Suggested Reading

Bowes, *Land Too Good for Indians.*

Green, *The Politics of Creek Removal.*

Miles, *Ties That Bind.*

Norgren, *The Cherokee Cases.*

Perdue and Green, *The Cherokee Nation and the Trial of Tears.*

Questions to Consider

1. How did the Cherokee engage in nation building? Why do you think their assertion of a sovereignty equal to that of the United States was not enough to prevent removal?

2. What do you think of the positions taken by the Ridge and Ross parties? Would it be fair to characterize one as pro-Cherokee sovereignty and the other as anti-Cherokee sovereignty?

NATIVE TRANSFORMATIONS ON THE GREAT PLAINS

Lecture 11

One of the most indestructible myths about Native America involves "the West"—a world of cowboys, wagon trains, and Native American warriors. This is the West of the colonial imagination, but this lecture offers a different perspective. Focusing on the Plains, we'll begin by exploring its formation in the colonial imagination during the early 19th century through Lewis and Clark's so-called voyage of discovery. Then, we'll change the perspective and arrive at a different way of seeing the Plains. Focusing on the theme of transformation, we'll explore an area that Lewis and Clark couldn't see—a West that wasn't a West at all, at least not for the indigenous peoples who saw it as the center of their universe.

Lewis and Clark's Voyage of Discovery

❖ Following on the heels of the Louisiana Purchase in 1803, President Thomas Jefferson commissioned Lewis and Clark to make an expedition. They were to prepare the way for a savage land to be incorporated into a civilized nation.

❖ The Corps of Discovery set out from St. Louis in May 1804—onboard a keelboat and canoes—and followed the Missouri River to Mandan villages, near what is today Bismarck, North Dakota. They traveled across the Bitterroot Mountains to the Pacific Coast in 1805 and then back to St. Louis in 1806.

❖ Lewis and Clark took many notes; made maps; drew pictures of Indian people, technology, and material culture, as well as plants and animals; and collected flora and fauna. Through an ethnocentric lens, the Corps of Discovery saw what they considered to be "backward" peoples

Thomas Jefferson

inhabiting an "untamed" and "unchanging" wilderness that the United States believed itself destined to possess.

❖ Indeed, common rituals involved in Lewis and Clark's encounters with Indians involved the giving of "peace medals," proclamations that the land now belonged to the United States, and assertions that President Jefferson would henceforth be their "father." All these actions were, of course, rituals of possession.

The Plains

❖ Taken as a whole, the Plains extends from the Upper Mississippi River Valley to the Rocky Mountains and from the Saskatchewan River to the Rio Grande. Within it are both the Prairie Plains to the east and the High Plains to the west.

❖ The Prairie Plains includes the tall-grass prairie on either side of the Mississippi River Valley and along the Missouri River. It can be contrasted with the more arid, short-grass prairies of the High Plains. The High

Plains extends from approximately the 100th meridian westward to the Rocky Mountains.

- ❖ Contact with Europe contributed to changes on the Plains.
  - ❭ Over the course of the 18th century, the Spanish established missions, settlements, and slave-raiding and trading networks through the Southwest and California. The French had forts, trading posts, and population centers along the Mississippi River Valley and the Gulf of Mexico. The English moved into the northern interior above the Great Lakes and engaged in trade along the Pacific Coast. Later, the Russians established a presence in the Gulf of Alaska.
  - ❭ It might seem that these newcomers were too far away to have any impact on the Plains, but that isn't the case. The vast indigenous trade networks that already extended across much of Native America meant that reverberations were felt far beyond the immediate sites of contact.
  - ❭ Everything from metal tools and woven cloth to alcohol and captives traveled along these old trade networks and were incorporated into American Indians' lives. Three elements that drove much of the change during the 18th century were guns, horses, and diseases.

Guns, Horses, and Diseases

- ❖ The guns the French first traded to the Anishinaabeg above the Great Lakes eventually arrived on the Plains through Hidatsa and Mandan trade centers. Their villages, located along the Missouri River in present-day North Dakota, served as important centers of exchange between Prairie and High Plains people.
  - ❭ From there, the Cheyenne introduced guns deeper into the Plains by way of trade with the Arapaho.
  - ❭ Meanwhile, traders based in St. Louis channeled guns onto the Plains through the Osage, Wichita, and Caddo.

- ❖ A similar dynamic fueled the spread of horses over the course of the 18th century.
  - ❭ Spanish horses were traded from Mexico and Texas to the Apache and, from there, were channeled through the Pueblo to the Ute and

Shoshone, and then to the Nimi'ipuu, Blackfeet, and Crow. To the east, the Wichita and Pawnee traded horses to the Caddo.

> In the heart of the Plains, the Comanche, who adopted horses and moved into the region during the 18th century, traded with the Kiowa Apache, who carried horses to the Arapaho, and northward to the Mandan, Hidatsa, and Arikara living in sedentary villages along the Missouri River.

> Horses fundamentally changed Indians' lifeways, worldviews, and means of social organization. They enabled increased mobility and, with their greater carrying power, allowed larger tepees and more extensive home furnishings. These, in turn, contributed to the development of elaborate status cultures, as horses became a new standard of wealth. Over time, horses were woven into the religious beliefs and rituals associated with war. Both combat and hunting became more lethal and efficient.

❖ But it wasn't just trade goods, guns, and horses that were moving through the Plains with transformative consequences through the 18th century. So, too, were Native peoples.

> Among the most powerful recent arrivals in the southern Plains were the Kiowa, Apache, and Comanche.

> The Kiowa were pushed out of the Black Hills area in present-day Wyoming and South Dakota by the Lakota and Cheyenne in the late 18th century. This led them to venture onto the southern Plains, where they built a way of life predicated on raiding, trading, and hunting bison.

> The Comanche, after their arrival during the 1730s, pushed the Apache (who had established their presence earlier) deeper into New Mexico and Texas and allied themselves with the Kiowa.

> The Comanche then turned to building what historian Pekka Hämäläinen refers to as an "empire" on the southern Plains, by virtue of their skills as raiders, traders, and diplomats as well as their access to guns through the Caddo and Wichita.

> To the north, the Cheyenne and Lakota established positions of prominence in the High Plains, having made their own westward

sojourns from the Great Lakes region over the course of the 18th century.
   > After battling with the Anishinaabeg and Cree over hunting grounds near the headwaters of the Mississippi River, the Lakota moved onto the Plains, pushing out the Omaha, Otoe, Missouria, Iowa, and Cheyenne. And by the late 18th century, they obtained guns and horses from the Arikara and emerged as an equestrian bison-hunting people.
   > To the east of the Lakota were the other two divisions of the Sioux: the Nakota and Dakota, who remained in the Prairie Plains.

- If horses, guns, other trade items, and peoples were moving through the Plains at accelerated rates before Lewis and Clark, so, too, were waves of diseases, including smallpox, cholera, and measles.
   > The horses that allowed people to travel on and expand existing trade routes with greater speed and over greater distances were among the engines propelling diseases. So, too, were the development of new trade routes, increased commercial exchange, more frequent raiding, and intensifying warfare, combined with the accelerated movement of peoples and competition over resources.
   > The impact of diseases was devastating. Population loss was commonly 30 to 50 percent and was often even higher among the relatively sedentary peoples of the Prairies.

Native Reaction to Plains Transformations
- In the 1780s, a Cree elder and smallpox survivor named Saukamappee, who lived among the Blackfeet, dictated a story of horses, guns, germs, and war on the northern Plains. Much of the story occurred near the Red Deer River, which joins the Bow River in southern Saskatchewan.
   > Saukamappee's narrative recounts an event that probably took place around 1781, as the Pikuni sought to rebuff the Shoshone. By this time, the Pikuni had not only secured horses but also possessed superior firepower by virtue of their access to guns and steel weapons.
   > The Pikuni scouts spotted a large Shoshone camp. When they attacked it the next day, they found, "There was no one to fight with but the dead and the dying." By taking back to their camp the tents

and personal possessions of their enemies, Saukamappee and the other men unwittingly spread smallpox among their own people.
> Although we don't know how many lives were lost, the death tolls were often very high. The effect of this biological disaster may well have been more destructive than any form of warfare they had ever seen.

❖ The narrative of Saukamappee offers a fascinating window into how Native people experienced and made sense of such diseases as smallpox. So, too, do the winter counts kept by Plains peoples.
> Winter counts are history books. They feature glyphs, or pictures, that mark a significant event in the life of a community during each year, measured from the first snowfall to the next year's first snowfall.
> Winter counts typically (but not always) begin in the center and spiral outward in a counterclockwise direction. Each glyph serves as a mnemonic device, helping those trained to remember them to recount the history of their people.
> As the end of a year approached, the community's elders met to discuss what had happened since the first snowfall. One event was chosen as means of remembering the entire year, and the year was given that name. It was the responsibility of the keeper of the winter count to paint the glyph on a buffalo hide (though sometimes, later, on paper or cloth) and to remember the history associated with it.
> The Lone Dog Winter Count, from the Yanktonai Nakota, is one example. The count records 70

years of Yanktonai history, and as we move from the center outward, we can see signs of all the transformations in Native lives taking place throughout the Plains before (and after) Lewis and Clark made their so-called discoveries. We encounter glyphs representing dead warriors (symbolizing increased tribal warfare), smallpox, horse theft, whooping cough, measles, the coming of white soldiers, warfare, the forging of peace, unusual astronomical events, and more.

❖ The Americans and all that they carried were not so much "new" to the peoples of the Plains as they were "next." And despite the profound disruptions they inaugurated, Native people still found ways to make the unfamiliar familiar, to transform even as they were being transformed. Yet as the 19th century would demonstrate, these mutual transformations on the Plains were far from over.

Suggested Reading

Calloway, ed., *Our Hearts Fell to the Ground*.

Fenn, *Encounters at the Heart of the World*.

Hämäläinen, *The Comanche Empire*.

Hoxie and Nelson, eds., *Lewis & Clark and the Indian Country*.

Salish-Pend d'Oreille Culture Committee, Elders Cultural Advisory Council, and Confederated Salish and Kootenai Tribes, *The Salish People*.

Questions to Consider

1. How did the introduction of guns, germs, and horses transform the lives of Native peoples on the Plains? How did American Indians transform the introduction of guns, germs, and horses?

2. What insights do we gain into how Native people made sense of the transformation of the Plains through Saukamappee's account and the Lone Dog Winter Count?

Lecture 12: INDIANS, MANIFEST DESTINY, AND UNCIVIL WARS

The decades before the American Civil War were defined by competing non-Native visions of expansion. The pervasiveness of non-Native assumptions can be found in the idea of Manifest Destiny, which held that expansion was part of a providential mission in which civilization would triumph over savagery. The U.S. government used treaties with tribal nations to pave the way for expansion. Treaties secured land cessions, extinguished Indian title, established forts and trading posts, and defined the boundaries of reservations. But what meanings did American Indians assign to the years leading up to the war, to the war itself, and to the war's repercussions? This lecture addresses those questions.

Nisqually People

* Between 1854 and 1855, Washington State's territorial governor, Isaac Stevens, conducted a treaty-making campaign throughout the Pacific Northwest and Plateau. Eleven hastily concluded treaties, forged in the context of huge multi-tribal councils, effectively ceded most of the land in the Pacific Northwest and Plateau to the United States.

* Along the banks of Medicine Creek, in the Washington Territory, on December 26, 1854, about 600 Nisqually, Puyallup, and Squaxin Island Indians met with a treaty commission headed by Washington's territorial governor, Isaac Stevens.

* An arrogant man who looked at the recognition of tribal sovereignty as beneath the dignity of the United States, Stevens adopted bullying command-and-obey tactics during the treaty negotiations, an extension of his own belief in Manifest Destiny. He influenced the selection of who

would represent the Indians at the council, and it wasn't clear whether they understood what they were agreeing to.

- Nonetheless, through the Treaty of Medicine Creek, Native people lost approximately 2.2 million acres, including vitally important fishing sites and prairie lands. The Nisqually were left with only a small 1,280-acre reservation on thickly wooded land, with no access to fresh water or the prairies.

- Leschi, a respected Nisqually headman, initially followed the path of accommodating the presence of non-Native newcomers. He was among the leaders chosen by Stevens to represent the Nisqually at the Medicine Creek Treaty.

- Although there is an X on the treaty that purportedly indicates his assent, Nisqually oral tradition holds that Leschi didn't sign it. Indeed, he refused to acknowledge the terms of the treaty, taking particular issue with being forced to remove to the small reservation identified in it. What's more, Leschi apparently threatened war if Stevens wouldn't renegotiate, and he left the treaty grounds before the signing took place. The X, then, may have been forged.

- Tensions grew in the months after the parlay at Medicine Creek and erupted in war in late 1855, when a party of militiamen traveling through Nisqually land was ambushed and two of them were killed. An eyewitness claimed Leschi took the life of one of them.

- The fighting reached a climax in March 1856, leaving the Nisqually defeated. In November 1856, Leschi was brought into custody, tried in a civilian court, and found guilty of murder. Despite his insistence that he wasn't present at the skirmish that led to the death of the two militiamen, Leschi was executed on February 19, 1858.

- The Nisqually were not, however, completely without redress. Article 6 of the Medicine Creek Treaty allowed for a "replacement reservation," which they secured in January 1857. It provided for about 4,700 acres straddling the Nisqually River and allowed them to continue a way of life that would have been virtually impossible otherwise.

- The Nisqually provide a different perspective on the 1840s and 1850s, years that are too often seen only through the lens of sectional crisis. The case study also demonstrates the consequences of the North and South's shared vision of establishing American Empire in the West.

- How does attending to the experiences of Native people change the way we think about the Civil War years themselves?
    - First of all, about 20,000 American Indians enlisted in either the Union or the Confederate armies between 1861 and 1865.
    - In the Carolinas, the Catawba and the Eastern Band of Cherokee Indians served as soldiers of the Confederacy. They did so as a means of protecting their own rights, sovereignty, and territory—not for love of the Confederate States.
    - In contrast, the Lumbee Henry Berry Lowry lashed out at White supremacists in Robeson County, North Carolina, who tried to force the Lumbee to serve the Confederacy during the Civil War.

The Lumbee

- By the 1850s, the General Assembly of North Carolina categorized citizenship by race and voided marriages between "whites" and "free persons of color" to the third generation. Both of these policies disenfranchised Native people, including the Lumbee. But that did not stop the state government from conscripting Lumbees during the Civil War.

- At home, the Lumbee endured violence directed at them by North Carolina's Home Guard, but Lumbee Henry Berry Lowry returned violence for violence, and as Union General William Sherman's army prepared to move across the Lumber River, the Lumbee assisted Union soldiers who had escaped from Confederate prisons.

- The raids that Lowry carried out culminated in a seven-year war against white supremacy and made him a legend.

The Cherokee

- For the Cherokee, who had been forcibly removed from the Southeast to the Indian Territory during the 1830s, the American Civil War contributed to one of their own.

- For the Confederacy, the Indian Territory was important for its resources. The farms, plantations, and ranches provided beef, hides, horses, and grain. Further, the Confederacy hoped the tribal nations there would provide troops to defend its far western borders.

- It seems to make little sense that Indians would fight on either side (especially for the Confederacy), given how badly they had been treated during the removal crisis of the early 19th century. As a result of the government's previous action, the Cherokee divided internally over the question of whether to ally with the Union or the Confederacy or to remain neutral.

- Principal Chief John Ross, who had guided the Cherokee Nation through the removal crisis and the ensuing period of rebuilding the nation, initially advocated for neutrality. He believed nothing could be gained from becoming involved in the war.

- After the Union abandoned their forts in the Indian Territory in 1861, however, Ross concluded a treaty with the Confederacy, and the Cherokee National Council issued a formal declaration of war against the United States in October 1861.

- In March 1862, the Union defeated a Confederate force supported by a Cherokee contingent at the Battle of Pea Ridge in northwest Arkansas. A few months later, Ross, who switched his allegiance once more to the Union, was arrested in his home by the Sixth Kansas Cavalry and, along with his family, went into exile.

- Meanwhile, Stand Watie, a member of the pro-removal faction during the 1830s and a perennial foe of John Ross, became the principal chief of the pro-Confederate government in August 1862.

- Commanding the Cherokee Mounted Rifles, Watie commenced a civil war within the Cherokee Nation that saw the burning of the capital buildings at Tahlequah and John Ross's home at Park Hill.

- The Civil War proved tremendously consequential for the Cherokee Nation. Even with John Ross restored as principal chief, the Cherokees faced a punitive peace in the Treaty of 1866 with the United States. The treaty included land cessions, the forced acceptance of railroad rights-of-way through their nation, the emancipation and enfranchisement of their former slaves, and the relocation of other tribal communities within their lands.

Dakota Conflict

- The Dakota were the easternmost division of the Sioux, with homelands located in what is today southwestern Minnesota. From August through September 1862, these homelands became a battlefield.

- At the heart of the Dakota Conflict were gross violations of the treaties of Traverse des Sioux and Mendota. Originally signed in 1851, they included land cessions, the establishment of a reservation along the Minnesota River, and guaranteed annuities in cash and food.

- Congress, before ratifying these treaties, struck from them the guarantee of reservation lands. White settlers soon encroached, and the Dakota grew dependent on predatory traders. The presence of assimilation-minded missionaries and inept government agents deepened the crisis, and the Dakota became polarized, leading them back to the treaty table in 1858. There, they were forced to accept another land cession (for which they were not paid fair-market value).

- By 1862, the Dakota had fallen into abject poverty, starvation, and dependence; tensions climaxed in August. Fighting raged for two months, leaving hundreds of soldiers, white civilians, and Dakota people dead.

- The tide turned in favor of the United States when President Lincoln charged General John Pope to deliver a decisive blow to the Dakota, which he did at the Battle of Wood Lake in late September 1862.

- The fallout from the Dakota Conflict was as horrific as the battles themselves. After 1,200 Dakota men, women, and children were taken prisoner, about 800 Dakota warriors surrendered. In a farcical mass trial in the fall of 1862, 303 Dakotas were sentenced to death for crimes ranging from rape to murder.

- President Lincoln, however, commuted many of their sentences. Nonetheless, the "Great Emancipator" signed the order condemning 38 Dakota men to be hanged in the largest mass execution in U.S. history.

Sand Creek Massacre

- The discovery of gold along the Front Range of the Rocky Mountains in Colorado in 1858 brought with it a tidal wave of non-Indian settlers. Soon, conflict erupted, especially as non-Natives encroached on land set aside for the Cheyenne and Arapaho through the 1851 Treaty of Fort Laramie. By 1861, through the Treaty of Fort Wise, the Cheyenne and Arapaho had their lands reduced to a useless parcel called the Sand Creek Reserve, near Fort Lyon, Colorado.

- Within a few years, Cheyenne warriors known as Dog Soldiers lashed out at the non-Native invaders. They did so with the conviction that they had not consented to the treaty and, therefore, were not beholden to it.

- In the fall of 1864, a Cheyenne leader named Black Kettle moved his band to Sand Creek, believing that they would avoid getting caught in the ongoing hostilities. Black Kettle even raised an American flag overhead, along with a white flag to signify peace and friendship. Nonetheless, Colonel John Chivington led the Third Colorado Cavalry in an attack of Black Kettle's camp on November 29, 1864.

- About 270 of his people were massacred by 900 soldiers. Black Kettle survived and chose the path of accommodation and treaty making once more. He moved his people into Oklahoma Territory, only to be butchered there by General George Custer and the Seventh Cavalry at the Washita River four years later.

The Diné

- In the Southwest, the Diné, or Navajo, also fought to preserve their homeland and way of life. To stabilize the New Mexico Territory, consisting of present-day Arizona and New Mexico, and to stymie Confederate incursions, the United States set out to force the Diné to accept a reservation away from their ancestral lands.

- In 1863 and 1864, Kit Carson conducted a campaign of total war against the Diné. A brutal invasion of the Diné stronghold in the summer of 1863 brought the Diné to the brink of starvation and compelled them to surrender.

- By 1864, the U.S. military inaugurated a forced march to an internment camp in a barren land called Bosque Redondo, near Fort Sumner, New Mexico. Between 1864 and 1868, approximately 8,000 Diné made the

400-mile march. This forced removal claimed the lives of more than 200 men, women, and children.

- ❖ At Bosque Redondo, the Diné endured malnutrition, disease, bad water, drought, and raids from the Comanche and Kiowa. Yet the Diné held fast and fought back, securing a treaty in 1868 that allowed them to return to their homelands.

- ❖ "The People still remember those dark years with pain and bitterness," Diné historian Jennifer Nez Denetdale writes of this ordeal. And yet, even as they mourn, she adds, they celebrate "the courage and resilience of their grandmothers and grandfathers."

Suggested Reading

Anderson, *Kinsmen of Another Kind.*

Blee, *Framing Chief Leschi.*

Hauptman, *Between Two Fires.*

Iverson, *Diné.*

Kelman, *A Misplaced Massacre.*

Questions to Consider

1. What is Manifest Destiny, and how did it shape federal Indian policy?

2. How do the case studies presented in this lecture broaden our conception of the Civil War and the larger era of which it was a part? Why do you think we tend to think of it only as an event that involved the North and the South and took place largely in the East?

Lecture 13: NATIVE RESISTANCE IN THE WEST, 1850s–1870s

During an 1868 treaty council, Alexander Gardner took a photograph of an American Indian woman with six white men, some wearing suits and others in military uniforms. All are identified by name, except the person at the center, referred to as an "unidentified Arapaho woman." This photograph is significant because it captures visually the idea that Native people were "becoming surrounded" during the latter half of the 19th century. It's also significant in that it renders Native people anonymous. In so doing, it serves as a metaphor for how Native perspectives are too often ignored. In this lecture, we'll locate Native people at the center of the defense of the northern and southern Plains from the 1850s through the 1870s.

The Northern Plains

- Although the end of the American Civil War opened a new chapter in the history of the Plains, much of the preparatory work for expansion was done during the 1850s and early 1860s.

- At the Treaty of Fort Laramie in 1851, the United States tried to clear the way for expansion by convincing the Lakota, Nakota, Dakota, and others to live in peace with one another and to stay within prescribed territories. According to the treaty, the Sioux territory covered about 134 million acres.

- U.S. treaty commissioners insisted that non-Indians be allowed to travel along the overland trails through Indian Country and secured permission to build more roads, as well as military forts and trading posts, along them. In return, Native people were promised protection from those who brought trouble into their country, while both sides agreed to provide restitution should there be conflict. Finally, the government pledged annuities of $50,000 per year for 10 years, to take the form of food and farm implements.

❖ But the United States did even more than sign treaties that defined more restrictive boundaries, acquired tribal land, and established rights-of-way and forts. In 1862, Congress passed attractive measures that encouraged westward migration for non-Indians. By 1890, the number of U.S. citizens residing west of the Mississippi River was 8.5 million.

Complicating Factors

❖ The influx of non-Indians into the West was fine by many Plains people—as long as they kept on moving, but of course, they didn't. The newcomers hunted on tribal lands without permission, and their livestock consumed precious spring grasses. They also introduced diseases, and the increased traffic on overland trails running through tribal hunting grounds drove the bison herds farther away.

❖ Contrasting ideas about political organization and authority also came into play. Impatient U.S. treaty commissioners arbitrarily appointed "head chiefs" to sign on behalf of "the tribes" as if they were nation-states. Native communities didn't see things the same way.
  > For instance, the Lakota, one of the three divisions of the Sioux Nation, actually consist of seven tribes, or *oyate*. Although extended family groups within the *oyate* might cooperate with one another to hunt, trade, and raid their enemies, they were considered politically autonomous, and there was no overarching governing or representative structure for the Lakota as a whole.
  > Some *oyate* agreed to the terms of the 1851 Treaty of Fort Laramie, and some didn't. For the Lakota, only the people from the bands whose leaders assented to the treaty could be seen as beholden to it.

❖ Another complicating factor was the increase in frequency and severity of fighting among Native peoples on the Plains in the late 18th and early 19th centuries, in large part because of the introduction of horses, guns, and diseases. A disagreement over the distribution of the annuities called for in the treaty made matters worse.

Violence on the Plains

❖ The Plains contains a vast diversity of people, and each of these nations adopted different strategies to deal with the expansion of the American Empire. For the Lakota, one incident in particular proved decisive in setting the stage for a 20-year defense of their land and way of life. This incident, which took place in mid-August 1854, involved the killing of a cow owned by a Mormon traveling along the Oregon Trail.

❖ The commander of the fort demanded that the cow's owner be paid $25 and that its killer, High Forehead, be turned over to federal troops. Conquering Bear, the Brulé leader, declined, pointing out that High Forehead was Miniconjou, and Conquering Bear lacked authority to make the man do anything.

❖ The fort's commander dispatched a military detachment outfitted with two howitzer cannons and led by Lieutenant John Grattan, but Grattan and his detachment were wiped out.

❖ The next year, the U.S. Army launched a horrific campaign that left 86 Lakotas dead. Sensing how dangerous the situation had become, the

Lakota organized a council that brought together between 5,000 and 10,000 Lakotas near Bear Butte.

❖ The council agreed that those who wanted to accept treaty annuities could stay and do so. Others would move into the bison range west of the Powder River in northeastern Wyoming and into the Black Hills. The Black Hills were of particular importance because the Lakota considered the area to be their place of origin.

❖ By the mid-1860s, the Bozeman Trail became the focal point of conflict. When the United States began constructing military forts along it, the Lakota, Northern Cheyenne, and Northern Arapaho made it known that they considered the construction in clear violation of the Treaty of Fort Laramie. They prepared to defend their lands and ways of life.

❖ Between 1866 and 1868, this intertribal alliance scored a series of dramatic victories against the U.S. Army and played a decisive role in bringing the United States back to the treaty table.

The Treaty of Fort Laramie

❖ The terms of the 1868 Fort Laramie Treaty speak to the importance of the December 1866 victory. The affirmation of Lakota land claims, the abandonment of the Bozeman forts, and continued tribal access to traditional hunting grounds were all remarkable, albeit temporary, testaments to tribal power on the Plains.

❖ Yet many Lakota, Cheyenne, and Arapaho refused to sign. They disagreed with the land cessions that reduced the territory originally demarcated by the 1851 Treaty of Fort Laramie, and they refused to accept reservation life.

❖ Although the Oglala leader Red Cloud signed and abided by the terms of the treaty, he later acknowledged that he felt betrayed. Other Lakota, including the Oglala warrior Crazy Horse and the Hunkpapa holy man Sitting Bull, rejected the treaty.

- Over the next few years, the United States declared that Lakota in the unceded areas were under military jurisdiction, allowed for the expansion of the Northern Pacific Railway through these same lands, and sent a military expedition under the command of General George Custer into the Black Hills to confirm the discovery of gold there.

- The U.S. government attempted to strong-arm the Lakota into relinquishing their claim to the Black Hills and, in January 1876, issued an ultimatum: Any Lakota who did not return to the reservation would be considered hostile.

Greasy Grass

- On June 25, 1876, Custer led an ill-fated attack on encampments along the Greasy Grass River. Several thousand Lakota, Cheyenne, and Arapaho were ready for them, and in the short run, the results were devastating for the United States.

- Yet if the Battle of the Greasy Grass—or Little Bighorn—represented a stunning military victory for the Lakota and their allies, it also signaled a turn toward their defeat.

- Under the strain of U.S. military harassment and deprivation, Lakota camps started to come apart. Families were forced to decide whether to remain with their relatives and starve or return to the Great Sioux Reservation and adjust to a radically different way of life.

Bringing in Crazy Horse

- In the wake of Greasy Grass, non-Indians wanted to tell a story that revolved around "bringing in Crazy Horse." But that isn't how the Lakota made sense of what happened in the winter of 1876 to 1877. Through the narrative of George Sword—an Oglala member of the agency police force on the Great Sioux Reservation—we encounter a different telling.

Among the holdouts in the Powder River Country was Crazy Horse, but he was murdered in the summer of 1877; the monument was begun in 1948.

- Sword was, indeed, part of a delegation sent into the Powder River Country to persuade the holdouts to surrender and return to Fort Robinson. But Sword does not focus his narrative on "persuading Crazy Horse to surrender." Instead, his story is about an attempt to heal a rift that was tearing the Oglala people apart. Unfortunately, the process grew more difficult in the spring of 1877.

- The holdouts in the Powder River Country did, indeed, return in May of that year, but Crazy Horse was murdered at Fort Robinson four months later. Sitting Bull's band came back in 1881, but his continued resistance to federal attacks on the Lakota way of life contributed to his own death in 1890.

- All the while, Congress followed through on its threats, taking that which the Lakota refused to give. In 1877, clearly in violation of the 1868 Treaty of Fort Laramie, federal legislation arbitrarily took from them the sacred Black Hills. The 152-million-acre Great Sioux Reservation had, in the span of 16 years, been reduced to fewer than 15 million acres.

Southern Plains

- A similar story played out on the southern Plains, where Southern Cheyenne, Southern Arapaho, Comanche, Kiowa, and Apache engaged in a massive treaty council with U.S. peace commissioners, much like the one that took place at Fort Laramie.

- The Medicine Lodge treaty council was a divisive moment. As we saw on the northern Plains, many bands within the tribes that were party to the treaty opposed its terms and, therefore, did not consider themselves bound to it.

- After the desperate winter between 1867 and 1868, many of the Comanche and Apache who had taken up residence on the reservation moved onto the Plains to hunt bison and raid cattle and horses. The federal army responded with a campaign that climaxed in the massacre of Black Kettle's village of Cheyenne along the Washita River in November 1868.

- Making the situation worse, the completion of the transcontinental railroad in 1869 effectively divided the once-massive bison herds on the Plains. It also contributed to their systematic slaughter.

- Through the early 1870s, Comanche and Kiowa forces struck out at bison hunters in the Texas Panhandle in an attempt to preserve Native ways of life.

- The U.S. Army retaliated with a multipronged offensive. The fighting reached a climax during the Red River War between August and December of 1874. Nine months later, the Natives surrendered.

- By the end of the 19th century, Plains people were, indeed, "becoming surrounded" by an expanding American Empire. But even in these darkest hours, they remained very much at the center of a struggle that was far from over.

Suggested Reading

DeMallie, "'These Have No Ears.'"

Hämäläinen, *The Comanche Empire*.

Isenberg, *The Destruction of the Bison*.

Marshall, *The Journey of Crazy Horse*.

Ostler, *The Plains Sioux and U.S. Colonialism*.

Questions to Consider

1. How did Native and non-Native people approach treaty making differently? Where in the lecture do you see the consequences of those differences?

2. How does the George Sword account narrate the events following the Battle of the Greasy Grass (or Little Bighorn) differently from standard accounts? What implications might these differences have for comprehending other pivotal events in American Indian history?

Lecture 14: THE LAST INDIAN WARS?

In the collections of the Smithsonian Institution's National Museum of the American Indian in Washington DC, you can find a revolver associated with the legendary Modoc leader Captain Jack, a Whitney rifle and glass-beaded leather gun case, a Winchester repeating rifle, an iron pipe tomahawk owned by the legendary Nimi'ipuu leader Chief Joseph, and Springfield and Whitney rifles that belonged to the legendary Chiricahua Apache leader Geronimo. The word "legendary" here purposefully underscores conventional stories associated with these "tragic heroes" who led their "doomed people" in the last Indian wars of the late 19th century. However, we will locate all these figures and their people at the center of a fuller, more complex, and unfinished story.

Native California

❖ American expansion and empire building brought incredible cruelty and violence to the central and northern parts of Native California during the mid- to late 19th century. After the discovery of gold during the late 1840s and California statehood in 1850, incidents of genocide and enslavement—along with the spread of diseases—devastated indigenous populations.

❖ Indeed, they were a part of the structural and systematic destruction of Native societies undertaken by the state of California from the date of its inception. The first elected governor characterized the state's conflict with Indians as a "race war," and the state issued federally backed bonds to fund militias formed to kill Native people.

- In response, some Native Californians engaged in treaty making, hoping to protect their land base, access to hunting and gathering sites, and water rights. Influenced by the lobbying of representatives from California, however, the U.S. Senate failed to ratify any of these treaties, thus making them invalid.

- Typically defined as "cheap labor" or indentured servants, California Natives endured gross exploitation. The inappropriately named Act for the Government and Protection of Indians in 1850, for instance, essentially legalized Indian slavery and the theft of Native lands.

Modoc Nation

- Numbering about 700 people and located near Tule Lake and the Lost River in northern California and southern Oregon, the Modoc were spared the worst consequences of colonial settlement until the 1850s and 1860s, when non-Native settlers began encroaching on Modoc land by way of the Applegate Trail, which led to gold fields in southern Oregon.

- In the early 1850s, the Modoc defended themselves against an invasion of miners and settlers. In response, California's militia conducted a

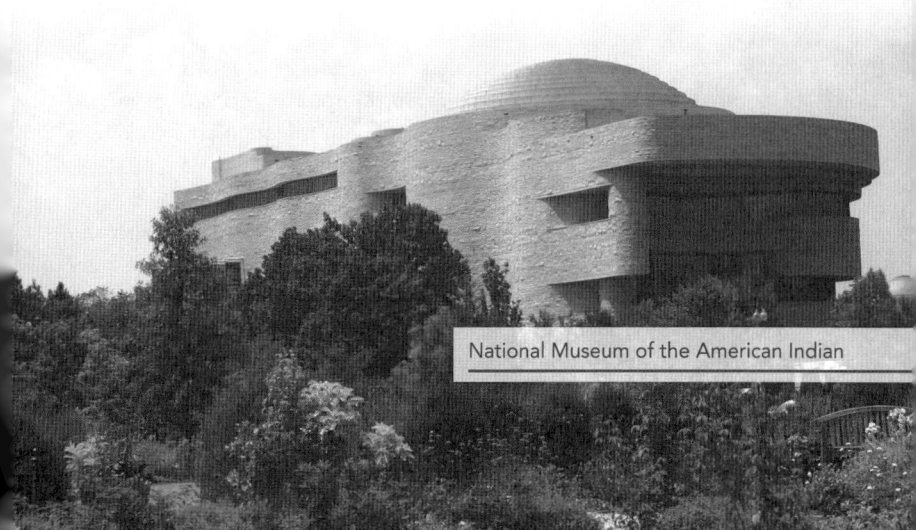

National Museum of the American Indian

devastating campaign that culminated in the massacre of 50 Modoc people during what was supposed to be a peace parley.

- In 1864, the Modoc signed a treaty that required them to move to the Klamath Reservation in southern Oregon. There, without proper food, clothing, or shelter, the Modoc suffered. The following year, 300 to 400 Modoc decided to return to their ancestral lands.

- Some of them followed Kintpuash—a man non-Indians called Captain Jack—who moved in and out of mining communities and had been a part of Modoc efforts to resolve their differences with non-Indians diplomatically. But he had also lost family, including his father, to the fighting of the 1850s.

- Kintpuash well understood that the Modoc were living in a world that offered few opportunities to find common ground with non-Natives. Nonetheless, Kintpuash, having returned home, focused on building peaceful relations and petitioned the federal government for a reservation.

- But conflict arose with non-Indian ranchers, who now considered the Modoc to be "trespassing" on their land; by the early 1870s, the federal government sent the army in to force the Modoc to return to the Klamath Reservation. Federal troops arrived at Kintpuash's village along the Lost River in late November 1872. When some Modoc resisted being disarmed, fighting broke out, leaving several soldiers dead.

- As Kintpuash's people fled, settlers simultaneously attacked the village of another Modoc named Hooker Jim. Kintpuash and approximately 150 Modoc men, women, and children sought refuge in an area known as the Lava Beds.

- In early January 1873, the U.S. Army surrounded and attacked the Modoc. The Modoc not only held their ground but also dealt the army a stinging defeat. Over the weeks and months that followed, Kintpuash engaged in negotiations with a federal peace commission, culminating in a series of talks in March and April. Alfred Meacham headed the

U.S. commission, assisted by General Edward Canby. A Modoc woman named Winema—or Toby Riddle—served as an interpreter.

- The Modoc were divided. Some, aligned with Kintpuash, wanted to continue to press for the establishment of a reservation in their homeland. Others, associated with Hooker Jim, believed that it was too late for diplomacy.

- When the peace commissioners insisted that the Modoc would not only have to surrender to the U.S. Army but also move to a new reservation in Arizona, Oklahoma Indian Territory, or southern California, Kintpuash relented to the pressure exerted by Hooker Jim and others. During yet another council on April 11, 1873, the Modoc delegation attacked the federal officials, killing Canby and wounding Meacham.

- The army eventually compelled Kintpuash to surrender. He and five others were convicted of murder and hanged at Fort Klamath on October 3, 1873. The federal government shipped the Modoc survivors to the Quapaw Indian Agency, located in northeastern Oklahoma and used as a place to forcibly relocate more than 20 tribal nations.

- Typically, the promised provisions didn't arrive, and many Modoc died in Oklahoma. Although some stayed, 51 others convinced the federal government to allow them to return to the Klamath Agency in 1909.

Nimi'ipuu (Nez Perce)

- The homeland of the Nimi'ipuu, or Nez Perce, included a vast area in southeastern Washington, northeastern Oregon, and parts of western Montana and Wyoming. By the 1850s and 1860s, the federal government's constant pressure to cede land to make way for westward expansion divided the Nimi'ipuu into treaty and non-treaty bands.

- In late May and early June 1855, the Nimi'ipuu negotiated the Nez Perce Treaty with Washington Territorial Governor Isaac Stevens.

> The Nimi'ipuu relinquished their claim to about 5.5 million acres of land, while retaining another 7.5 million acres and reserving the right to hunt, fish, and gather in the ceded areas. In return, the Nimi'ipuu received compensation in the form of cash payments, provisions, schools, and instruction in farming and various trades.
> This strategy prevented the United States from following through on an earlier proposal that would have forced the Nimi'ipuu to live among the Walla Walla, Cayuse, and Umatilla on the Umatilla Reservation in Oregon Territory.

❖ In 1863, a few years after the discovery of gold, the federal government returned with still more demands. Some Nimi'ipuu signed the treaty, which required the Nimi'ipuu to relocate to a smaller reservation in the Clearwater Valley in Idaho. The majority of Nimi'ipuu, however, neither signed nor acknowledged the legitimacy of the 1863 treaty.

Defined by great ridges, massive boulders, and intricate caves and caverns, the Lava Beds were highly defensible; they also contained a number of sacred places for the Modoc.

- In 1871, the leader of the Nimi'ipuu in the Wallowa Valley, Old Joseph, passed away, and his son, also named Joseph, honored his father's last request that they remain in their homeland, although more white settlers flooded into the area.

- In May 1877, the army informed the younger Chief Joseph that his people's time in the Wallowa Valley had run out. The Nimi'ipuu would have to resettle on the Lapwai Reservation in Idaho or be deemed hostiles.

- During the exodus to the Lapwai Reservation, the Nimi'ipuu skirmished with settlers. Joseph responded by leading his people into White Bird Canyon to give them time to decide how best to move forward. To his dismay, in mid-June, a parley with a force of pursuing U.S. troops went horribly awry, and fighting erupted.

- At this point, the Nimi'ipuu concluded that the only way to survive as a people would be to seek refuge in Canada. By August 1877, a second detachment of American troops from Fort Missoula, Montana, caught up with the Nimi'ipuu near the Big Hole River. Under the command of Colonel John Gibbon, the soldiers inflicted high casualties on the Nimi'ipuu.

- The escapees first headed in a southeasterly direction before veering northward toward Canada. In the Bears Paw Mountains, approximately 40 miles from the border—and freedom—the Nimi'ipuu were once again surprised by a detachment of U.S. soldiers.

- On September 30, the soldiers attacked the haggard Nimi'ipuu encampment, driving away their horses and forcing them to dig in for a final battle. The Nimi'ipuu fought hard but couldn't hold on.

- Before laying down arms, however, Joseph and other leaders secured from Colonel Nelson Miles the assurance that the Nimi'ipuu would be able to return to their homeland. Instead, they were forced into exile—ultimately to a desolate northeast corner of the Indian Territory.

- In 1884, after many years of campaigning, Joseph and his band secured a transfer. But it wasn't to their home. Approximately half went to the Lapwai Reservation in Idaho. Joseph and the rest went to the Colville Reservation in Washington Territory. Joseph died and was buried at Colville in 1904.

The Chiricahua

- The Chiricahua are one of several politically autonomous Apache people. They occupied what is today southern Arizona and New Mexico. They further subdivided into four bands; within these bands were matrilineally defined local groups of approximately 30 extended families.

- Geronimo, or Goyathlay, "the one who yawns," was born into the Bedonkohe band during the 1820s. Like Kintpuash and Joseph, he came of age in a world that was growing increasingly perilous. Mexican and American authorities routinely vilified the Apache, characterizing them as a threat to civilization. From the 1860s to the end of the 1880s, Geronimo came to symbolize the Chiricahua struggle to maintain their independence and way of life.

- During the early 1870s, the U.S. government attempted to force all of the Apache—about 8,000—to accept reservations. Beginning in the fall of 1872, the Chiricahua Reservation was established in southeastern Arizona.

- Subsequent raids into Mexico by the Chiricahua led federal officials to consolidate virtually all the Western Apaches at the San Carlos Reservation in 1874. San Carlos was already overcrowded, and it was an arid wasteland. Geronimo was forced to move there in 1877. Unwilling to accept the indignities of reservation life, Geronimo led small bands of Apaches into the Sierra Madre Mountains in Mexico on three occasions.

- The Apaches' last flight to freedom began in May 1885. Geronimo and more than 100 men, women, and children were hounded by American troops. After peace negotiations fell apart at the last minute in March

1886, the United States replaced an army officer named George Crook with Colonel Miles.

- Finally, on September 6, 1886, Geronimo surrendered at Skeleton Canyon in southeastern Arizona. Rather than returning to San Carlos, the Chiricahua were put on a train and, like the Modoc and Nimi'ipuu, sent into exile.

- Geronimo and the Chiricahua were imprisoned in Fort Marion, near Saint Augustine, Florida. There, they joined other Apache who, despite remaining at San Carlos, had been deemed hostiles and were also incarcerated.

- In 1894, the Apache were moved again, this time to Fort Sill in present-day southwestern Oklahoma, where Geronimo lived out his remaining years.

Suggested Reading

Ball, *Indeh.*

Cothran, *Remembering the Modoc War.*

Hurtado, *Indian Survival on the California Frontier.*

Jacoby, *Shadows at Dawn.*

West, *The Last Indian War.*

Questions to Consider

1. There is no question that the last decades of the 19th century witnessed endemic warfare across the trans-Mississippi West. But do these case studies reaffirm or challenge the idea that this period saw the last Indian wars?

2. In the wake of the fighting, many of the Modoc, Nimi'ipuu, and Chiricahua Apache were imprisoned, relocated far from their homes, or both. Why?

Lecture 15: CHALLENGING ASSIMILATION AND ALLOTMENT

As we've seen, sometimes, everyday items tell the most profound stories. Consider a paper ration ticket that an American Indian could use to claim beef, beans, corn, flour, salt, and other supplies each week on the reservation. These everyday items tell stories that defy the notion that American Indian history ended in the late 19th century with the collapse of military resistance. Taking inspiration from such objects, this lecture explores how American Indians continued to think about and adjust to the extraordinary challenges and changes they faced during the late 19th and early 20th centuries. Without question, the greatest challenge was the federal government's deliberate effort to dismantle reservations and obliterate tribal cultures through allotment and assimilation.

The Situation in Native America

- The situation in Native America was grim as the 19th century came to a close. The American Indian population had collapsed. A pre-European contact population estimated at between 7 and 18 million people had been reduced, according to federal reports, to perhaps 250,000, by the turn of the century. It seemed as though poverty, dependency, and forced confinement on reservations were becoming a way of life.

- That the United States abandoned treaty making in 1871 underscored the idea of an irrevocably diminished tribal sovereignty. Past treaties remained in force, but the federal government now referred to treaties as "agreements," a reflection of its inclination to no longer look on tribes as nations of equal stature.

- For non-Indians, the primary question was: What shall become of those few American Indians who remained? Because Native people understood the past and present differently, they asked a different question: How do we reconcile ourselves to this "civilization" that has surrounded us?

Formal Education

- Merrill E. Gates, a man who had shaped federal policy as a member of the Board of Indian Commissioners offered one answer: assimilation. And the two primary vehicles for realizing this transformation were formal education and land allotment.

- When it came to using schooling to remake the individual and collective identities of American Indians, no one stood taller than Captain Richard Henry Pratt.
  - A career military man, Pratt styled himself a progressive when it came to race. Not unlike Gates, Pratt believed that assimilation would prove the racial equality of Indians—an idea that was radical to a non-Indian population that generally assumed Indians were biologically inferior.

At the end of the 19th century, bison herds that once numbered 30 million were reduced to perhaps 1,000.

- > But Pratt also believed that one would have to "kill the Indian" to "save the man." In other words, Pratt was convinced that American Indians would have to die culturally in order to survive physically.

- In 1875, Pratt undertook the Fort Marion experiment in Saint Augustine, Florida, where he oversaw 72 Kiowa, Apache, and Cheyenne prisoners from the southern Plains wars.

- To change the mind, according to Pratt, one must begin with the body. Thus, the prisoners had their hair cut, and their traditional clothes were exchanged for military uniforms. Pratt also fostered acquisitiveness, encouraging the prisoners to create and sell to non-Indian tourists artistic representations of their experiences within their communities and at war with the United States.

- In 1879, Pratt opened the Carlisle Indian Industrial School in Carlisle, Pennsylvania. An extension of the Fort Marion experiment, it operated on a much larger scale and targeted children, rather than adults.
  - > On their arrival, Native young people were forced to trade in their familiar clothing for woolen military uniforms and "proper" dresses. Their hair was cut and restyled.
  - > Although the instruction was primarily vocational, students also took classes in history and civics, home economics, art, music, and language.
  - > In other words, students had their political identities reoriented and their histories rewritten; the United States was to be "their nation."

Land Allotment

- Congress also devised legislation to carry out the second means for defining how Indians would be incorporated into the United States: land allotment.

- Massachusetts Senator Henry L. Dawes was the architect of the General Allotment Act of 1887, and he expressed the view that private property would serve as a panacea for the so-called Indian problem. From this point of view, communal values were preventing Indians from becoming productive, acquisitive, and "intelligently selfish"—and communally owned land sustained these values. Dawes and the advocates of allotment concluded that reservations should be eliminated.

- ❖ The General Allotment Act featured three major components: defining (taking a census of Native communities), dividing (subdividing reservations into family parcels), and divesting.
  - › It was common for non-Indians to believe that communal ownership of land for Native people was wasteful and unproductive.
  - › Thus, in the wake of defining and dividing, something miraculous happened: There appeared to be huge swaths of "surplus" land that Indians didn't need!
  - › The government then opened this surplus land to non-Indians, who, it was thought, could make better use of it, anyway.

- ❖ Allotment promised to make everyone a winner. White people gained access to more land. And Indians, heretofore trapped in a supposedly savage state, could generate wealth from private property.

- ❖ The endgame in the allotment process was citizenship. The Board of Indian Commissioners stated the belief that tribal values, lifeways, and communal land ownership were un-American. Private property, however, offered an alternative path.

- ❖ After a 25-year period of trusteeship (a term that was shortened in succeeding legislation), American Indian allottees were to receive "fee patents" for their land. Fee patents took the land out of trust and made it taxable and available to be sold. Once this happened, Indian allottees became full citizens of the United States.

- ❖ Unfortunately, allotment unleashed a tidal wave of corruption, collusion, fraud, theft, and even murder throughout Indian Country. And, as could be expected, through allotment, Native people lost millions of acres of land.

- In addition to destroying the tribal land base, allotment was about reconfiguring the way people thought about themselves as individuals and in relation to others.
  - During census taking, the federal government assigned "degrees of Indian blood" that served as an imposed definition of identity. The "blood quantum" of a person was then correlated with his or her "competence."
  - High degrees of Indian blood made people "more Indian" and less competent. Lower degrees of Indian blood made people "less Indian" and more competent. This was racism at its worst.

Results of Education

- Returning to Fort Marion and the Carlisle Indian Industrial School, let's think about what they meant to three people: Wohaw, Daklugie, and Luther Standing Bear.

- A veteran of the Red River War during the 1870s, Wohaw—a Kiowa—was probably 20 years old when he was transferred from the Indian Territory to Fort Marion in Florida. During his time there, he created a drawing called *Wohaw in Two Worlds* that seemed to present a typically bifurcated view of identity. But when we look closely at Wohaw's art, we can imagine a person adept at accommodating to new circumstances, rather than someone who felt compelled to abandon one identity for the sake of another.

- We gain similarly complex insights into the life of Daklugie—a Chiricahua Apache who fought against the U.S. Army during the 1870s and 1880s. Scarred by his experiences at Carlisle, Daklugie went so far as to abandon Asa, the name he was given there. We get the sense that Daklugie, like Wohaw, defined his encounter with assimilation on his own terms. Rather than accommodate, he flat out refused.

- Standing Bear, a Lakota, told yet another story. Named Plenty Kill and raised among the Oglala on the Great Sioux Reservation during the late 1860s and early 1870s, he described going to the Carlisle Indian Industrial

School as an act of bravery, but he didn't entirely reject Pratt's vision or the Carlisle experiment. Instead, as with Wohaw, he defined it on his own terms.

- Later in his career, Standing Bear joined Buffalo Bill's Wild West Show. This gave him the opportunity to earn money while traveling across the United States and Europe.
- He also began what would become a successful career as a writer, which included his now-classic 1928 memoir, *My People the Sioux*.

Results of Allotment

❖ Taken as a whole, allotment proved devastating. Yet some American Indians successfully adapted to individual ownership and profited from farming and leasing their lands. In fact, there were significant debates between those who wished to preserve traditional lifeways and those who enjoyed advantages through support from agency officials and, therefore, embraced so-called progressive opportunities.

❖ Other Natives selected contiguous allotments to preserve the integrity of extended kin groups or to use private property to escape the watchful eye of agency superintendents. This enabled Indians to continue traditional religious practices, such as the Sun Dance, as they came under attack during the early decades of the 20th century.

❖ Still others, such as Comanche chief Quanah Parker, devised strategies of accommodation and subversion that allowed his people to endure despite radically changed circumstances.

- As a judge on his reservation's Court of Indian Offenses, Parker protected traditional religious practices that he at least vocally opposed.

› Further, after initially resisting allotment because of the threat it posed to the ability of Comanches to lease tribal lands to Texas cattlemen, he came to see the threat in a different light. Rather than continuing his opposition, Parker represented his people in negotiations with the federal government to secure larger allotments, to demand just compensation for surplus lands, and to save half a million acres of the reservation from allotment.

Indian Adaptation, Persistence, and Survival

- The experiences of Wohaw, Daklugie, Standing Bear, and Quanah Parker are only a small part of a larger and more complex narrative of Indian adaptation, persistence, and survival. They remind us, in their own unique ways, that there was more to assimilation and allotment than a choice between Indian and white worlds, Native and non-Native cultures.

- In fact, we realize that the dilemmas of choosing between two worlds and two cultures were false ones. These binaries were only real in the collective imagination of non-Indians. Native people knew better.

- Remaining in the wake of allotment and assimilation were more questions: Could Native people, even in light of assimilation, be accepted as equal to whites? Could citizenship tolerate diversity and the possibility of dual national identities?

- Throughout the late 19th and early 20th centuries, dueling expectations about and answers to these questions continued. But one thing was clear: Native people refused the idea that assimilation was inevitable or even that they had to choose between "Indian" and "white" worlds.

Suggested Reading

Adams, *Education for Extinction.*

Child, *Boarding School Seasons.*

Hoxie, *A Final Promise.*

Lookingbill, *War Dance at Fort Marion.*

Standing Bear, *My People the Sioux.*

Questions to Consider

1. How did assimilation and allotment seek to remake American Indian identities? Did they have the impact that reformers intended?

2. How did such Native people as Wohaw, Daklugie, Luther Standing Bear, and Quanah Parker answer the question of what it would mean to belong as individuals, members of communities, and nations within the United States?

AMERICAN INDIANS AND THE LAW, 1883–1903

This lecture explores how, in the wake of the so-called last Indian Wars, Native people continued fighting for their rights and their land during the late 19th and early 20th centuries. But they fought on different ground and with different weapons. Among them was the legal system that had done so much to dispossess Native people. In 1823, Supreme Court Chief Justice John Marshall referred to this system as "the courts of the conqueror." Many Native people used these same courts to demonstrate that conquest was not complete. In this lecture, we'll focus on three cases that were decided between 1883 and 1903: *Ex parte Crow Dog*, *United States v. Kagama*, and *Lone Wolf v. Hitchcock*.

Ex Parte Crow Dog

- In the broadest sense, *Ex parte Crow Dog* revolved around the question of who had jurisdiction over murders committed within the boundaries of a reservation: tribal nations or the federal government. It was a question about the limits of tribal and federal power.

- At the local level, Bureau of Indian Affairs (BIA) agents exercised tremendous power, even making decisions about whether Native people could have access to their own money. Indian Affairs agents worked to undermine traditional leaders and imposed foreign systems of law and government. They even had their own police force staffed by people from the community they sought to control.

- Between 1851 and 1877, the Lakota land base was reduced by treaties, congressional acts, and allotment from more than 134 million acres to less than 15 million acres. Throughout this period, the Lakota were divided over how best to deal with non-Natives challenges. Some Lakota resisted militarily, while others chose an accommodationist path.

❖ The murder at the heart of *Ex parte Crow Dog* was a product of these divisions.
  › Quite intentionally, the agents on the Lakota reservations undermined the traditional pathways the Lakota used to gain status and authority.
  › At the same time, new avenues to gaining authority were opened, such as courting the favor of agency superintendents and serving on the agency's Indian police force.
  › As a result, tensions grew in Lakota communities. Among the 10,000 Brulé Lakota living in traditional camps around the Rosebud Agency, these tensions ended in murder.

❖ The Brulé chief Spotted Tail had fought against the United States during the 1850s but, by 1880, controlled the Indian police force. One Lakota who disagreed with Spotted Tail's strategy of accommodation was Crow Dog, a Brulé band leader who had twice served as captain of the agency Indian police and was clearly against accommodation.

Spotted Tail

❖ There appeared to be a personal dispute between Spotted

Lecture 16—American Indians and the Law, 1883–1903

Tail and Crow Dog in play, as well. The dispute ended with Spotted Tail being gunned down by Crow Dog in August 1881. The exact circumstances are murky, but the dictates of traditional Lakota justice kicked in.

- Rather than turning himself in to the BIA police, Crow Dog surrendered to another Brulé named Hollow Horn Bear. He gave the victim's family $600 in cash, eight horses, and one blanket. Under Lakota customary law, the matter was settled.

- But non-Indians, including the agency superintendent, demanded that American justice be exacted. Between September 1881 and March 1882, Crow Dog was apprehended, indicted, tried, and found guilty of murder in the district court of the Dakota Territory. He was sentenced to hang.

- The district court's ruling was affirmed in May by the territorial Supreme Court, and the case next went to the U.S. Supreme Court. In what at first appeared to be a stunning victory, a unanimous decision found in favor of Crow Dog. Customary law in cases arising between Indians on Indian land, the court held, was considered an "inherent attribute of sovereignty" recognized by treaties and could not be violated through the imposition of state or federal law.

- However, the Supreme Court rejected the rationale used to indict and find Crow Dog guilty because Congress had not expressly repealed customary law in cases involving Indians on Indian land.

- *Ex parte Crow Dog* left unanswered questions: Where did federal law begin and end? And what power did Congress have to decide that question—particularly if it meant diminishing tribal sovereignty?

United States v. Kagama

- The Major Crimes Act of 1885 defined the circumstances in which federal courts could intervene in crimes committed between Indians in reservation communities. This act identified a number of offenses, including murder, to be so serious as to give federal authorities concurrent jurisdiction. Was it within the power of Congress to legislate that or not?

- ❖ This question was at the heart of *United States v. Kagama*, another murder case, this one involving three Klamath men living in the Hoopa Valley Reservation in northern California.

- ❖ One of them, Kagama, wanted to build a house and inquired about securing legal title to a piece of land. However, Kagama's claim was disputed by another Klamath named Iyouse. In June 1885, Kagama and his son stabbed Iyouse to death. The murder became a test case for the constitutionality of the Major Crimes Act.

- ❖ The case was taken up by the U.S. Supreme Court in the spring of 1886, after both Kagama and his son were indicted for murder. In a devastating blow to tribal self-government, the Supreme Court upheld the constitutionality of the Major Crimes Act. In so doing, it conveyed three important ideas.
    › The decision perpetuated the illusion that as Native people became surrounded geographically and demographically, their systems of governance and social control were automatically diminished. In other words, the United States would not necessarily allow tribes to govern themselves or deal with their own local affairs in their own way.
    › The decision also justified the extension of concurrent federal jurisdiction over tribal communities by invoking the language of trusteeship and protection, as if preventing tribes from governing themselves was somehow a "duty." As bad as the decision was, *Kagama* did not deprive tribes of the power to try and punish the offenses enumerated in the Major Crimes Act. But it did say that the federal government could also assert jurisdiction.
    › Finally, the decision advanced an expansive definition of federal regulatory power known as plenary power. This doctrine held that Congress could legislate in any way that it deemed "beneficial" to tribes.

- Ironically, it was determined that because the murder had not taken place within the boundaries of the Hoopa Valley Reservation, the Major Crimes Act had no bearing, and the state of California declined to prosecute.

- But a potent precedent had been set, and more questions lingered: Where did the power invested in Congress end? What were the limits of guardianship? How far could Congress take the idea of "protecting" Indians and acting in their "best interest"?

Lone Wolf v. Hitchcock

- By the 1860s, beset by war and disease, the Comanche, Plains Apache, and Kiowa people faced increasing pressure to cede land. For example, the Little Arkansas Treaty of 1865 involved the cession of millions of acres of land stretching from present-day southern Colorado and eastern New Mexico through much of west Texas.

- The reservation accepted by the Kiowa and Comanche was never established, and two years later, they met with a peace commission established by Congress to negotiate treaties with the Plains tribes. The outcome of this massive gathering of nations was the Treaty of Medicine Lodge.

- In this treaty, the Kiowa, Comanche, and Apache signatories ceded all but 3 million acres of land located in present-day southwestern Oklahoma in return for annuities, schools, churches, assistance becoming ranchers and farmers, and protection from buffalo hunters.

- During the next few years, the federal government failed to follow through on the promised provisions, and the slaughter of the bison continued. With the bison depleted, the loss of their hunting grounds, and their mobility restricted, life became increasingly challenging for the Natives.

- After 1890, non-Indians flooded into the space defined as Oklahoma Territory, demands for allotment increased, and the movement for statehood gained momentum.

- In September 1892, federal negotiators, referred to as the Jerome Commission, were dispatched to secure the allotment of the Kiowa-Comanche-Apache Reservation—purportedly to "ensure civilization." The agreement, supposedly reached in October, called for the allotment of approximately 440,000 acres of reservation lands to 2,759 tribal citizens. Thus, 2 million acres magically became "surplus land" and ripe for non-Indian people's taking.

- A Kiowa leader named Mamay-day-te (also known as Lone Wolf the Younger or Elk Creek Lone Wolf) challenged the legitimacy of the agreement and resisted the federal commissioners' efforts to secure an allotment agreement.
  > Lone Wolf contended that the Jerome Agreement was fraudulent. This did not, however, stop Congress from passing legislation in 1900 to move allotment forward.
  > Citing the violation of the Treaty of Medicine Lodge, Lone Wolf sought an injunction in the courts in June 1901.

> In the meantime, allotment rolled on, with the survey of tribal lands beginning in August 1901.

- Lone Wolf turned to his nephew Delos to help him fight back. Born in 1870, Delos had attended the Carlisle Indian Industrial School from 1892 to 1896. He then returned to the Kiowa-Comanche-Apache Reservation, where he used his facility in the English language to combat the federal government's assault on Kiowa land.

- In January 1903, the justices handed down a unanimous decision. Endorsing *Kagama*'s definition of plenary power, the Court ruled that tribes were not independent nations but were, instead, dependents and in a state of pupilage.

- This was a crippling blow to tribal sovereignty. The decision meant that Congress could unilaterally act in a way that violated the sanctity of nation-to-nation agreements so long as it deemed the action to be in the "best interests" of tribal communities. It did not even matter whether the tribal community being acted upon agreed.

Case Studies in Defending Sovereignty

- Law played an integral role in the "surrounding" of Native America through the imposition of foreign ideas and institutions during the late 19th nineteenth and early 20th centuries. These Western ideas about law and justice served as the handmaidens of assimilation and colonial control by disempowering tribal institutions and treating Native people as incompetent in matters of jurisprudence.

- Through passage of the Major Crimes Act, Congress legitimated the extension of federal law into tribal communities, further threatening tribal systems of governance and justice. In addition, the Supreme Court invested Congress with potentially unlimited power with the meaning it assigned to the doctrine of plenary power.

❖ To be sure, power was shifting away from tribal governing institutions and systems of justice. And, not only that, but Native people were becoming estranged from the law itself. Yet in the context of the communities we've considered in this lecture, the struggle for justice continued, as did the assertion of the right to be self-governing.

Suggested Reading

Clark, Lone Wolf v. Hitchcock.

Harring, *Crow Dog's Case*.

Mathes and Lowitt, *The Standing Bear Controversy*.

Wilkins, *American Indian Sovereignty and the U.S. Supreme Court*.

Wilkins and Lomawaima, *Uneven Ground*.

Questions to Consider

1. To what extent do you think American Indians were successful in using the U.S. legal system to protect tribal sovereignty during the late 19th and early 20th centuries?

2. What is plenary power? Why, according to this lecture, should it not be seen as a sign of utter defeat for tribal sovereignty?

THE GHOST DANCE AND THE PEYOTE ROAD

Lecture 17

With military resistance no longer an option, many American Indians turned to the sacred to gain a sense of peace, place, harmony, balance, reconciliation, and belonging in difficult times. This lecture explores how that process took place in the context of the Ghost Dance and the Peyote Way during the late 19th and early 20th centuries. These were not, however, reactive movements born only of despair but positive assertions of survival, hope, and joy. Their syncretistic natures also suggest the ongoing connectedness and dynamism of Native cultures. The lecture concludes with a consideration of the Wounded Knee Massacre and the unintended consequences of assimilation.

Origins of the Ghost Dance

❖ The Ghost Dance movement began on the Walker River Paiute Reservation, in present-day western Nevada. Its originator was Jack Wilson, or Wovoka—the Ghost Dance Prophet—born during the mid-1850s.

❖ Orphaned at the age of 14, Wilson grew up and worked on the ranch of the devout Presbyterian non-Indian family that adopted him—hence the name Jack Wilson. He may have been called Wovoka ("Woodcutter") because he hired himself out to cut down stands of cedar and piñon pines to fuel the mining industry.

❖ On January 1, 1889, a day that saw an eclipse of the sun, Wovoka reportedly heard a great sound while chopping wood and, when he went to investigate, inexplicably collapsed and received a powerful vision.

❖ He was given knowledge of a dance—one that, if performed properly and coupled with righteous living, promised to cleanse the earth of whites and restore it to all Native people. The dance provided a pathway to healing, peace, satisfaction, and joy—and a means of reuniting with loved ones who had passed away.

Spread of the Ghost Dance

❖ The Ghost Dance spread quickly out of the Great Basin and into the northern and southern Plains between 1889 and 1890, facilitated by word of mouth and the railroads.

❖ Everywhere the Ghost Dance spread, different Native communities imbued it with particularized meanings and, in some cases, unique traits in relation to their own traditions and contemporary circumstances.

❖ That was certainly the case among the Lakota on the northern Plains, who also give us a specific perspective on why the Ghost Dance was so appealing to American Indians.
  › Sociologists use the term "anomie" to describe a feeling of disempowerment and purposelessness that is created when people can no longer attain accepted societal goals through accepted societal means. That's what was happening on reservations. Native people could no longer provide for themselves as they once had or practice the ways of life that the creator had given them.
  › In 1883, the Lakota held their last buffalo hunt and, in 1884, their last Sun Dance. The latter had brought all the Lakota together for courting and fun but had been outlawed by federal agents. As anthropologist Raymond DeMallie explains, the Sun Dance was "a real affirmation of Lakota identity and power, in both physical and spiritual senses."

❖ In 1888, the Indian Bureau agent at Pine Ridge expanded the assault on Lakota identity by prohibiting the use of ritual bundles, which were made by the Lakota when a person died.

- Further, the Lakota now had to participate in "ration days," when they gathered at the agency for distributions of beef, corn, flour, salt, coffee, and the like.

- The passage of an act in the spring of 1889 to further subdivide the Great Sioux Reservation into six smaller ones, thus opening still more land to non-Indians and making life more precarious for Lakotas, added insult to injury.

- This was the context into which the Ghost Dance was fitted and why its message was so appealing to Lakotas. They had seen the loss of autonomy and power. They had lost loved ones to disease and malnutrition. They had been attacked physically, culturally, and spiritually by soldiers, federal agents, and missionaries.

Outlawing the Ghost Dance

- In the late summer and early fall of 1890, Lakota emissaries, such as Kicking Bear and Short Bull, carried their own versions of Wovoka's teachings back to the Standing Rock and Rosebud Reservations, and Big Foot emerged as a central figure in the Ghost Dance movement at Cheyenne River. The Lakotas were ready to listen.

- As Wovoka promised, the Ghost Dance offered the Lakota peace, the restoration of balance, and the continuing integrity of Lakota lifeways. What's more, even as it represented something new, it was consistent with Lakota notions of power, or wakan, and religious expression.

- The Lakota also added their own elements to the Ghost Dance. For them, the restoration of human life depended on the restoration of animal populations, especially the bison. The Ghost Dance was appealing because it served as a ritual means of securing the return of the bison and, by extension, the health of the people.

- Yet many whites at the time—and no shortage of historians in later years—suggested that somehow the Lakota saw in the Ghost Dance an opportunity for violent retribution. They pointed to Lakota innovations, such as Ghost Shirts and Ghost Dresses, which were purportedly bulletproof, although this was not the case.

❖ For the Lakota, as for other Native people, Wovoka had provided the foundation for a doctrine of restoration and peace. They even held Ghost Dances on "Sabbath days" and invited agents to watch in hopes of fostering tolerance.

❖ It was the federal agents who created a climate of fear and hostility. In the fall of 1890, they first attempted to stop the dance by withholding rations; then, they outlawed the Ghost Dance; and finally, they demanded that federal troops be sent to the agencies.

Wounded Knee

❖ In November 1890, the first of about 5,000 soldiers arrived in Lakota country. Ghost Dance leaders and prominent supporters, such as the Hunkpapa Sitting Bull, were targeted for arrest. Many Ghost Dancers fled to remote villages or the Stronghold, a highly defensible position located in the Badlands.

Sitting Bull

- On the morning of December 15, 1890, an Indian police force surrounded Sitting Bull's home. During the arrest, the Lakota holy man, six of his people, and seven policemen were killed.

- Big Foot, the leader of the Ghost Dance at Cheyenne River, then set out with 350 Lakotas for Pine Ridge, where he hoped they would be able to avoid trouble. They were intercepted on December 28 by the Seventh Cavalry and escorted to a camp along Wounded Knee Creek. They awoke the next morning surrounded by soldiers and Hotchkiss guns.

- When the soldiers went to take their weapons, a shot rang out. The Seventh Cavalry, perhaps seeking revenge for the defeat they had suffered at the Battle of the Greasy Grass in 1876, unleashed its fury on the Lakotas. The camp was decimated. Lakota survivors sought refuge in a ravine and were killed there. Bodies were found miles from where the fighting started.

- Lakotas on Pine Ridge, including the holy man Black Elk, responded by donning their Ghost Shirts, taking up arms, and riding to defend their people. But soon they, too, returned to the agency. Nevertheless, if Wounded Knee became a shared symbol of suffering, it also became a shared symbol of the resilience of Lakota peoplehood.

The Peyote Road

- Another critically important pathway to peace, reconciliation, and belonging is known as the Peyote Road or the Peyote Way.

- Peyote is a small, spineless cactus native to northern Mexico and southern Texas. Non-Indians typically defined peyote as a "drug" because of its hallucinogenic properties. For this reason, missionaries and federal agents tried to stamp it out. But for followers of the Peyote Way, peyote was (and is) a sacrament, just like the bread and wine in the Christian tradition. In fact, some peyotists considered peyote to be the body of Christ.

- The Peyote Way took hold in Western Oklahoma by the late 19th century. And, like the Ghost Dance, the people who carried it from one community to the next took advantage of railroad networks and made innovations to the ideas, songs, and ceremonies.

- Two of the most important late-19th- and early-20th-century peyote roadmen (leaders of peyote ceremonies) were Quanah Parker, a Comanche, and John Wilson, a Caddo. Parker defined one of the mainstays of the peyote tradition, called the Half-Moon Way, while Wilson established the Big-Moon or Cross-Fire Way.

- One of the most important distinguishing features of these traditions was the degree to which Christianity and Christian symbols were woven into the meetings. Evidence of the multiple forms syncretism took in the Peyote Way can be seen in peyote songs and hymns, the content and form of prayers, and the integration of Christian and "American" iconography.

- The Peyote Way also came to include an artistic tradition filled with beautiful iconography and featuring adorned accouterments, including feather fans, water drums, and prayer staffs. Here, too, both Christian and American signs, such as the American flag, abounded.

- For practitioners, peyote was a means of communing with the sacred. It taught its followers how to "think good thoughts" and "know good from evil." The Peyote Way also underscored "right living" in the form of eschewing alcohol, infidelity, and fighting. But that did not stop Christian missionaries and federal agents from launching campaigns against it.

- Interestingly, Quanah Parker, who served as the Comanche's principal chief, actually welcomed the presence of missionaries, served on the Court of Indian Offenses, supported the leasing of tribal lands to ranchers, and spoke out against the Ghost Dance. One of the reasons, of course, was to protect the Peyote Way.

- When it came to time to fight openly, Quanah also accepted that challenge. As Oklahoma moved toward statehood in 1906 and 1907, Quanah was among the Indian delegates at the constitutional convention and advocated for the formal protection of their religious freedom.

- After Quanah's death in 1911 and a federal legislative assault, peyotists incorporated under the state laws of Oklahoma as the Native American Church in 1918. The reason for this was to give the Peyote Way standing as a legitimate institution in the eyes (and laws) of the majority society.

- Although the Ghost Dance and the Native American Church represented two of the most visible forms of turning to the sacred to find hope in an age of despair, they were by no means the only ones.
    - Among the Oto and Potawatomi, the Oto prophet William Faw Faw provided a compelling vision to guide the people into the future. In the Great Lakes region, the Ojibwe continued the Midewiwin tradition and the Dream Drum. In the Pacific Northwest, Native people continued to hold potlatches, while John Slocum, a Squaxin prophet, founded the Indian Shaker Church.

› Still other individuals moved into the world that was engulfing them, reimagining the meaning of Indianness in the process. Whatever path they chose, Native people refused the notion that Indians would soon be no more.

Suggested Reading

Andersson, *The Lakota Ghost Dance of 1890*.
DeMallie, "The Lakota Ghost Dance."
Neihardt, *Black Elk Speaks*.
Smoak, *Ghost Dances and Identity*.
Stewart, *Peyote Religion*.

Questions to Consider

1. In what ways did the Ghost Dance and Peyote Way serve as means of finding a sense of peace, place, harmony, and balance during difficult times?
2. Where do we see the unintended consequences of assimilation in the case studies of the Ghost Dance and the Peyote Way?

NATIVE AMERICA IN THE EARLY 1900S

Lecture 18

With the onset of the 20th century, Native people adopted new means of preserving, protecting, and reimagining their identities and communities. This lecture introduces the concepts of expectation, anomaly, and binaries of authenticity to provide a sense of the challenges they faced in attempting to do so. It then offers case studies of political figures, writers, intellectuals, performers, actors, filmmakers, painters, athletes, and laborers who actively engaged in a process of remaking their selves and their communities. In the process, they carved out new spaces for being Indian in the 20th-century United States.

Expectations

❖ The scholar Philip Deloria uses the word "expectation" to highlight the way the majority society thinks about what Indians look like, how Indians speak, and where Indians live.
  › During the early 20th century, popular expectations would have Indians wearing buckskins and feathers, using broken English, and living on reservations, for instance.
  › But what if Indians didn't fit these descriptions? What if an Indian wore an evening dress, spoke fluent German, or lived in Paris?
  › Deloria would say that members of the majority society would have to make a choice. They could dismiss the differences by deeming them anomalous, in which case the differences would simply reinforce their expectations. Or they could define the differences as unexpected, in which case the differences would cause them to reevaluate everything they thought they knew.

- Following the historian Paige Raibmon, let's envision the conventional wisdom according to a series of binaries that juxtapose that which is "authentic and Indian" and that which is "inauthentic and white."
    - To be "authentically Indian" was to be irrational, subordinate, rural, pagan, traditional, colonized, uncivilized, timeless, cultural, collective, static, and of the past.
    - To be "inauthentically Indian" was to be rational, dominant, urban, Christian, modern, a colonizer, civilized, historical, political, individual, dynamic, and of the future.

- For Native people, challenging expectations proved extraordinarily difficult because these binaries had become internalized by the majority society.

Challenging Expectations

- Perhaps the best—or, at least, the most visible—example of defying expectations through political action took place in the context of the Society of American Indians (SAI), which held its first meeting in Columbus, Ohio, on Columbus Day 1911. This was a powerful symbolic gesture, conveying that "discovery" had not led to disappearance.

- The members of the society included Native people from many walks of life, but the organization's leadership largely consisted of highly educated professionals, including academics, physicians, and lawyers. Often, they put their educations in off-reservation boarding schools and seminaries, colleges, universities, and medical schools to unexpected purposes.

- In the pages of their quarterly journal, they advocated for justice, democracy, the extension of full citizenship rights, and the reform (or abolition) of the Bureau of Indian Affairs.

- The SAI also insisted that Native people be treated as equals. They attacked racist imagery and derogatory depictions of Indians as monosyllabic, backward, and somehow less than human. They argued for education reform to train intellectuals, leaders, and skilled professionals.

- Although society members certainly advocated for treaty rights, they were divided over such issues as whether the sacramental use of peyote should be outlawed and whether the popular Wild West Shows were empowering to the Indians who worked in them, or whether they reinforced negative stereotypes and the perception of Indian wildness and savagery.

- With a central office in Washington DC, and a membership that exceeded 600, the SAI came to represent what scholars have called "the first modern intertribal political organization." And that's true. But the SAI was also the product of an evolving "pan-Indian" consciousness that had been in development for many years. The boarding schools founded in the late 19th century were among the forces that strengthened a shared identity predicated on shared experiences. And there were several attempts to form pan-Indian organizations before the SAI's founding.

- The early 20th century saw the founding of the Alaska Native Brotherhood and Alaska Native Sisterhood, the Indian Defense League of America, an organization of Plains peoples to defend tribal sovereignty, and the Black Hills Convention.
  > Tribal delegations constantly visited Washington DC, where they advocated for treaty rights, defended tribal lands and resources, and demanded justice in Congress and the courts.
  > What all this political activity had in common was the insistence that treaties, land and water rights, religious freedom, and traditional ceremonial practices were not things of the past.

Native Writers

❖ During the late 19th and early 20th centuries, indigenous writers, such as Sarah Winnemucca, Liliuokalani, Charles Eastman, Zitkala-Sa, and Arthur C. Parker, offered both overt and subtle critiques of the majority society through their memoirs, fiction, poetry, editorials, and academic writing.

❖ That was certainly true of Sarah Winnemucca, a Northern Paiute woman who offered a stinging indictment of the U.S. government and the hypocrisy of "civilization" in her 1883 autobiography, *Life among the Paiutes: Their Wrongs and Claims*.

❖ By the end of the 19th century, the process of incorporating indigenous people into the United States extended beyond reservation communities. And it proved most complete in the Hawaiian Islands, where an alliance of American missionaries and businessmen undermined the Hawaiian monarchy during the 1880s.
  › Liliuokalani, who became Hawaii's queen after her brother's death in 1891, continued the struggle for Kanaka Maoli, or Native Hawaiian, independence. In 1893, she was forced to relinquish her authority, but she didn't give up the fight.
  › Instead, over the next several years, she traveled to the United States and used the power of her voice and pen to lobby against the ratification of an annexation treaty. Moreover, she advocated tirelessly for a new Hawaiian constitution that would enfranchise the Kanaka Maoli and restore power to the monarchy.
  › In her 1898 autobiography, *Hawaii's Story by Hawaii's Queen*, Liliuokalani deployed (in ways surely unexpected by her audience) such concepts as citizenship, civilization, representation, international law, and Christianity in defense of Hawaiian nationhood.
  › U.S. President Grover Cleveland initially sided with her against the missionaries, planters, and American imperialists, but Liliuokalani still wasn't able to forestall annexation. When the United States went to war with Spain in 1898, American expediency trumped American values, and Hawaii was annexed.

- Another person who defied expectations with his writing was Dakota physician Charles Eastman. His 1916 memoir, *From the Deep Woods to Civilization*, presented a vexing narrative, one filled with dark ruminations on the arrogance and excess of industrial America, free-market capitalism, materialism and acquisitiveness, and (to the extent that it was used to legitimate these things) Christianity, which he likened to a "machine-made religion."

- Consider, too, Zitkala-Sa's piece "Why I Am a Pagan," which appeared in *Atlantic Monthly* in 1902. In this essay, Zitkala-Sa painted a portrait of hypocritical Christian missionaries and preachers (some of them Native), who seemed more concerned with right belief than right behavior. She offered an unexpected analysis of Native spirituality by suggesting that it brought her closer to God than Christianity ever could.

- Other writers, including the Seneca Arthur C. Parker, offered their own critiques by way of academic treatises. Parker was particularly adept at drawing on his expertise in ethnology, joining other anthropologists in attacking antiquated ideas that equated "racial inferiority" with "Indian blood."

Native Artists

- Probably the most popular form of entertainment relating to Native Americans at the end of the 19th century was Buffalo Bill's Wild West Show, a traveling performance featuring Indians who reenacted historical events, traditional life, and acts of skill.
  - At first glance, one might think that these spectacles—in which "real" Plains Indians acted out "real" moments in their own histories—were the height of exploitation.
  - But there was much more to the shows than that. Working for Buffalo Bill meant an opportunity to earn money, engage in practices the Indian Office was busily suppressing, travel, and serve as ambassadors for their people.

- By the early 20th century, a new entertainment medium—filmmaking—was quickly making headway even as the popularity of the Wild West Shows waned. And once more, Native people were at the center of it.

  Luther Standing Bear

  - One of the most successful Native actors of the period was Luther Standing Bear, a Lakota who had worked for Buffalo Bill. As an actor—whether as part of the Wild West Show or on film—Standing Bear clearly saw himself engaging in the politics of representation.
  - As president of the Indian Actors Association, Standing Bear insisted that Native actors play Native roles instead of the typical non-Indians in "brown face." He also served as an advisor to the era's leading Western filmmakers and pushed them to go beyond stereotypes.
  - Through the 1920s and 1930s, Standing Bear continued to engage in the politics of representation as the author of a classic memoir, *My People the Sioux*, and the hard-hitting *Land of the Spotted Eagle*.

- It's important to note that Native men and women didn't just act. The Ho-Chunk Nation actor Lillian St. Cyr (or Princess Red Wing), for instance, collaborated with her husband in many other aspects of filmmaking. Although they typically didn't make overtly political films, they—like Standing Bear—engaged in the politics of representation.

- Native people also challenged expectations about Indians in sports. Native athletes included Louis Sockalexis, John Meyers, and Charles Albert Bender, who all played professional baseball; Olympic winners Lewis Tewanima, Duke Kahanamoku, and Andrew Sockalexis; and Jim Thorpe, considered by many to be one of the greatest athletes of the 20th century.

- At the grassroots level, in reservation and non-reservation spaces, Native people carved out places for themselves on their own terms. This included engaging in ceremonial, religious, and social revivals, such as the potlatch or ceremonial giveaways in the Pacific Northwest, as well as innovations, such as the early development of powwow culture on the Plains.

- Further, Natives expanded their engagement in the market economy. This included cattle ranching among the Lakota, Ute, and Apache and craft production in the Southwest, as well as migratory labor in California, maple sugar-making among the Anishinaabeg, and lumbering among the Menominee and Klamath.

- Through the late 19th and early 20th centuries, then, American Indians were everywhere. And everywhere, American Indians defied the majority society's expectations and binaries of authenticity. As political actors, writers, cultural producers, athletes, and participants in the market economy, Native people reimagined Indianness by remaking a sense of self and community that should be seen as anything but anomalous.

Suggested Reading

Deloria, *Indians in Unexpected Places*.

Hoxie, ed., *Talking Back to Civilization*.

Raibmon, *Authentic Indians*.

Silva, *Aloha Betrayed*.

Troutman, *Indian Blues*.

Questions to Consider

1. What do we mean by "expectation," "anomaly," and "binaries of authenticity"? How did the individuals discussed in this lecture challenge them?

2. By adopting and deploying ideas, values, and concepts from the majority society, did American Indians challenge or reinforce its power over their lives?

AMERICAN INDIANS AND WORLD WAR I

Lecture 19

World War I and the New Deal created new spaces for American Indians to reassert their own ideas regarding citizenship and sovereignty amidst ongoing pressures to destroy tribal lands and identities. This lecture explores how World War I set the stage for a contest over the meaning of citizenship, and it considers the experiences of soldiers. From there, we delve into controversies over universal citizenship, tribal lands, and religious freedom during the 1920s.

A Dark Period

- The early 20th century was a dark period for many tribal nations—so dark, in fact, that one might wonder why American Indians would serve the United States in a time of war.
    - By the time World War I erupted in Europe in 1914, the tribal land base had been reduced by millions of acres, and the American Indian population had reached its nadir. The citizens of sovereign tribal nations had become "surrounded" by the laws, values, economy, and culture of a foreign majority society.
    - What's more, it wasn't clear whether tribal communities as separate nations would survive—that is, whether there was any place for them in "these United States."

- Allotment and assimilation—the dominant U.S. federal policies directed toward American Indians since the 1880s—advanced a vision for the future that we might call "the citizenship of sameness."
    - Allotment divided tribally owned reservation lands into individual parcels that American Indians were to own privately. At the end of a

"trust period," American Indian allottees were to become full citizens of the United States.

› Federal officials assumed that the special rights Indians retained as citizens of tribal nations would disappear along with communally held tribal lands.

❖ Cultural assimilation, which allotment fostered, took many forms, including schooling in Western ideas about gender and religion; vocational training; and the eradication of American Indian languages and cultures. The Bureau of Indian Affairs (BIA) promoted assimilation by disrupting the ability of tribal councils and business committees to be self-governing and by imposing Courts of Indian Offenses, used to punish Indian people for violating federally imposed laws.

Native Responses to World War I

❖ Based on all this, one might have expected a largely unsupportive Native response to American involvement in World War I, but that wasn't the case.

❖ On the home front, many Native people supported the war. They planted victory gardens; made contributions to the Red Cross, YMCA, and Salvation Army; and bought war stamps and about $25 million worth of Liberty Bonds. This giving is even more remarkable when juxtaposed with the rampant poverty in Native communities during these years.

❖ Men and women also served the United States as laborers, leaving their reservation homes in search of new work opportunities. They assembled military vehicles at the Ford Motor Company plant and worked at the Hog Island naval shipyard.

❖ Meanwhile, about 4 million acres of tribal and allotted lands were leased to non-Indians. On the Pine Ridge Reservation in South Dakota, for instance, the Lakota leased three-quarters of their rangeland so that non-Indians could graze cattle and sheep to produce beef and mutton to send overseas.

❖ Between 12,000 and 16,000 Native men and women also served in the armed forces. Despite the fact that many American Indians were not U.S. citizens and, therefore, not subject to selective service legislation, more than 17,000 registered for the draft. Another 3,500 volunteered to serve.

❖ The reasons American Indians gave for serving in the U.S. military provide windows into the multiple meanings they assigned to citizenship and sovereignty—both U.S. and tribal.
> Some American Indians probably saw themselves as patriotic Americans fighting for "their country."
> Still other Native people fought for "their country" while not conceiving of it as the United States at all. The Onondaga and Oneida of the Iroquois Confederacy took this stance when, in July 1918, they declared war on the Triple Alliance as independent nations and agreed to fight as allies, rather than as subjects, of the United States.

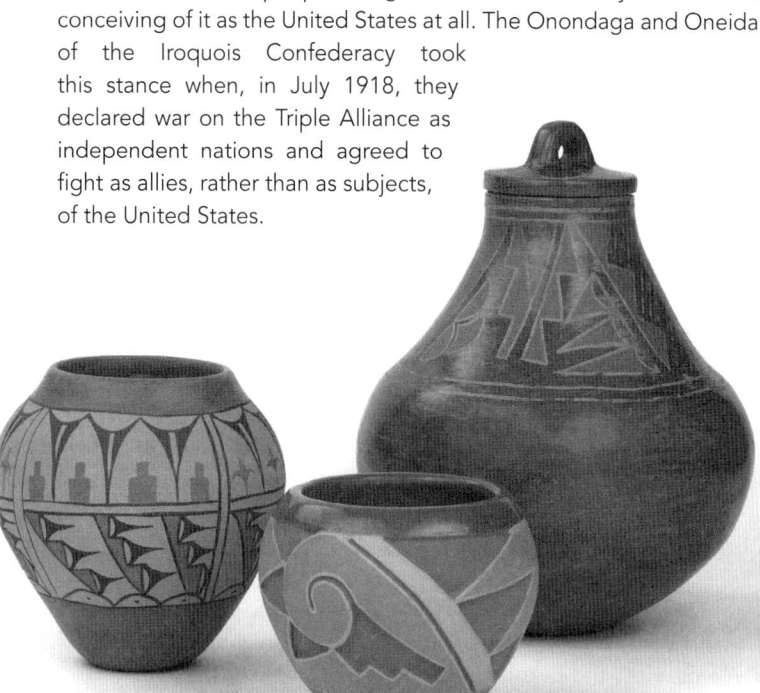

- › Still another group fought for the land. A Yakama veteran explained that his people possessed a love for their homeland so strong that it allowed them to overcome feelings of mistrust toward the U.S. government.
- › And there were surely American Indians who joined the service because it afforded an opportunity for excitement and adventure or to bring honor to themselves and their families.

❖ However, there was open resistance to the draft among the Pueblo, Hopi, and Navajo in the Southwest; the White Earth Ojibwe in Minnesota; the Muscogee Creek in Oklahoma; and the Iroquois peoples in New York State. Conflict over allotment—and the threat that the destruction of communal land ownership posed to control over tribal resources—informed much of this dissent.

Code Talking

❖ During World War I, individuals from six tribal nations—the Cherokee, Cheyenne, Comanche, Osage, Yankton, and Choctaw—engaged in code talking (sending and receiving cryptographic messages). Of these, the Choctaw language served as the basis for the development of a special vocabulary.

❖ The idea for the Choctaw Telephone Squad originated in October 1918, when American forces were pinned down by a German attack at St. Etienne. The Germans had proven adept at tapping American telephone lines, effectively compromising their ability to reposition troops and artillery and to coordinate attacks.

❖ By chance, an officer in the 142nd Infantry overheard two soldiers speaking with each other in Choctaw. This, in turn, led to the plan to use the language over the field telephone system to safely redeploy troops. Eventually, 18 Choctaws used their language to great effect during the final campaign of the war.

Consequences of Native Service in the Military

- ❖ Native soldiers fought in all the major American offensives from May through November 1918. Although many of them demonstrated valor, American Indian service was often rendered as particular and unique—with problematic consequences.

- ❖ For example, American Indians—because of the way they were viewed by their commanding officers—were not infrequently put in dangerous situations. Because of their supposedly "innate sense of direction," "stealthiness," and "warlike temperament," Indians were dispatched as scouts, runners, and snipers—all of which carried especially high casualty rates. Native bravery in these and other roles was also portrayed as evidence of Indian "savagery."

- ❖ Race thinking played a second role in defining American Indian service—one that created a pernicious catch-22. For many outsiders, Native patriotism was simultaneously perceived as an abandonment of tribalism and acquiescence to being "conquered." Service, in other words, became both a marker of Indians' innate savagery and their acceptance of assimilation.

Postwar Native Experiences

- ❖ With military service being characterized in such restrictive ways, what place could Native people expect to have in the postwar United States? What implications would the war have for ongoing contests over the meaning of citizenship and sovereignty? These questions were taken up by a generation of American Indian intellectuals that came to the fore during the early decades of the 20th century.

- ❖ Many of the most outspoken figures were affiliated with the Society of American Indians (SAI), which took stands on a wide variety of issues, but the organization focused its attention on raising awareness of the deplorable state of reservations, revealing corruption in the BIA at the local and national levels, and advocating for U.S. citizenship.

- Arthur C. Parker, the Seneca anthropologist, and a Yavapai physician named Carlos Montezuma both held that U.S. citizenship and reform of the BIA were, if not prerequisites for serving in the war, necessary outcomes.

- In 1919, the year after World War I ended, Congress responded to such appeals by extending the opportunity to apply for U.S. citizenship to all American Indian veterans. Then, in 1924, Congress passed the Snyder Act, which made all American Indians citizens of the United States.

- U.S. citizenship, however, wasn't a panacea. A monolithic "citizenship of sameness" that denied Native people their rights as citizens of tribal nations was, for some Indians, a problem, not a solution. Moreover, many other Native people looked at the Snyder Act as an unwanted imposition that violated their sovereignty.
  - Members of the SAI, for instance, expressed their position on these matters as world leaders gathered for the Paris Peace Conference between January 1919 and January 1920. The SAI based its vision for the future of Native America on U.S. President Woodrow Wilson's vision for the postwar world.
  - Alluding to the president's Fourteen Points, Dakota physician Charles Eastman and Yankton Sioux writer Zitkala-Sa emphasized the importance of guaranteeing the rights of self-government and self-determination for all the "little peoples" and "small nations" of the world, including tribal nations.
  - The Iroquois and the Pueblos of the Southwest rejected U.S. citizenship.

- Throughout the late 19th and early 20th centuries, Pueblo people engaged in a desperate battle to save their homelands from non-Indian squatters, many of whom claimed to have purchased land from individual Pueblos.
  - In 1922, New Mexico Senator Holm Bursum proposed a bill tilted in favor of non-Pueblo claimants and rushed it through the Senate without a hearing.

- > In response, Pueblo delegates met in Santo Domingo to operationalize the All Indian Pueblo Council. The organization included an alliance with sympathetic non-Indians, and together, they successfully prevented the Bursum Bill from becoming law.
- > During the controversy over the Bursum Bill, the Pueblo drew distinctions between U.S. and tribal citizenship, as well as U.S. and tribal sovereignty. Moreover, they offered a vision in which all of them could coexist.
- > According to this vision, the Pueblo (and, by extension, other Native people) would not sacrifice their rights as citizens of their own nations or their ways of life on the altar of the citizenship of sameness.

- Throughout the early 1920s, contests over the meaning of citizenship and sovereignty continued. This can be seen no more clearly than in the BIA's attempts to ban Indian dances. The agency issued circulars directing agency superintendents to withhold rations and imprison Indians who violated bans on dances and other ceremonial practices that were considered "degrading" or "immoral."

Outcomes of the World War I Experience

- By the mid-1920s, the assault on Pueblo land rights had abated. The attempts to ban Indian dances were in retreat. Native people secured U.S. citizenship, but notably, not at the expense of tribal citizenship.

- At the same time, allotment and assimilation were coming under determined attack, and the federal administration of Indian affairs received such withering criticism that reform appeared imminent. But what would these reforms look like? What changes would they bring?

- The answer to these questions and the implications they had for citizenship and sovereignty, remained uncertain even as an era of greater uncertainty began.

Suggested Reading

Britten, *American Indians in World War I*.

Hoxie, ed., *Talking Back to Civilization*.

Krouse, *North American Indians in the Great War*.

Rosier, *Serving Their Country*.

Wenger, *We Have a Religion*.

Questions to Consider

1. What impact did World War I have for Native people at home and abroad? How did it become integral to ongoing struggles over sovereignty?

2. How did Native Americans understand their service in the war? How does that complicate our understanding of patriotism and love of country?

Lecture 20: MAKING A NEW DEAL IN NATIVE AMERICA

It's common to associate the Great Depression with the stock market crash of October 1929 and the beginning of aggressive economic and political reforms with the inauguration of President Franklin D. Roosevelt and the New Deal in 1933. But both of these oversimplify matters. By 1929, much of rural America was already in dire economic straits, and there were many calls for federal reform through the 1920s. Of course, American Indians didn't just sit back and watch this happen. Before the stock market crash and New Deal, Native people were vocal critics of the ways in which the Bureau of Indian Affairs (BIA) oversaw the federal government's obligations to tribal communities, including health, education, welfare, and economic development.

Native Political Action

- Through the early decades of the 20th century, Native political action took many forms, including establishing business committees to run tribal affairs and sending delegations to Washington DC to meet with federal administrators and testify before Congress. Native people also organized locally, regionally, and nationally.

- At the national level, the Society of American Indians (SAI), founded in 1911, advocated for citizenship rights, treaty rights, and federal reform. The SAI also supported the movement to have the U.S. Court of Claims opened to all tribes and bands.

- By the early 1920s, the SAI went into eclipse. Individuals within the SAI, however, continued to carry considerable influence after the organization disbanded in 1923.

- For example, among the founders of the SAI was Laura Cornelius Kellogg, an Oneida woman who devoted her life to increasing tribal self-sufficiency through communal land ownership and economic enterprises. She believed reservations should not be incorporated into the United States and that they were worth fighting for.
- In 1920, she published *Our Democracy and the American Indian*, a defense of reservations and a call for the preservation of protectorate status for tribes vis-à-vis the federal government.

❖ Other former SAI members added their voices through such organizations as the American Indian Defense Association and through advisory committees, including the Committee of 100 and the Meriam Commission.
- A number of SAI veterans were involved in the Committee of 100, established in the spring of 1923. The committee also included Henry Roe Cloud, a Ho-Chunk minister, educator, and intellectual from Nebraska.
- In December 1923, the Committee of 100 presented President Calvin Coolidge with a report. The committee criticized the federal government's administration of Indian affairs, called for more study of the effects of peyote to deflect attacks on it by the BIA, and advocated opening the Court of Claims to tribal nations.

❖ The committee also paved the way for more exhaustive and influential studies, including the Brookings Institution's Meriam Commission, which began its work in 1926. Henry Roe Cloud served as one of the coauthors of the commission's report on the administration of Indian affairs.
- Published in 1928, the Meriam Report attacked the BIA for its failures in education, health care, and economic development. It was also critical of incorporation through allotment, portraying it as a contributing factor to the dire circumstances found across Indian Country.
- Although the Meriam Report stopped short of refuting the assimilationist objectives of Indian policy, it did advance a vision of corporate land ownership similar to Kellogg's.

The Indian New Deal

- By the time of the stock market crash in 1929, then, calls for reform from Indian Country had already gained momentum. Natives and non-Natives turned back assaults on tribal land rights and religious freedom and dealt a significant blow to allotment and, to a lesser extent, assimilation. The loss of tribal sovereignty was not an acceptable cost of U.S. citizenship.

- This activism prepared the ground for the Indian New Deal, which Roosevelt inaugurated as part of the larger New Deal.

- To oversee the Indian New Deal, Roosevelt turned to John Collier as his commissioner of the BIA. Collier had already established himself as an outspoken advocate of Native rights. Between 1933 and 1934, Collier worked with some of the best legal minds to devise the Indian Reorganization Act (IRA).

- Introduced to Congress in February 1934, the IRA sought foremost to end allotment. In its place, it proposed fostering self-government through the adoption of tribal constitutions and bylaws, reconsolidating the tribal land base, and promoting economic development by calling for a $10 million revolving loan fund for tributes that adopted constitutions. (This amount was later reduced to $2.5 million.)

- In the spring of 1934, with Henry Roe Cloud as one of his main emissaries, Collier convened a series of congresses across Indian Country to explain the IRA and get feedback from tribal communities.

- The IRA became law in June 1934; 181 tribes with a population of 129,750 people voted to accept it. Seventy-seven tribes, with a population of 86,365, rejected it. Later iterations extended its provisions to Oklahoma Indians and Alaska Natives.

The Diné

- Among the tribal nations rejecting the IRA were the Diné. Their decision reflects the complex entanglement of history, other controversies, and Collier's visions for reform.

- In 1868, Diné leaders successfully negotiated a treaty that provided for the return to their ancestral homeland from the desolate Bosque Redondo Reservation. There, the Diné restored connections to family and place and rebuilt the nation.

- Central to Diné identity, sustenance, and lifeways were their livestock, especially goats and sheep.
  - In 1868, the Diné had 14,000 sheep. By 1929, sheep and goats numbered 1.3 million. But soil erosion, drought, hard winters, and the intrusion of non-Native ranchers conspired against the Diné. And in 1933, the Soil Erosion Service and BIA strong-armed Diné leaders into accepting forced stock reduction, arguing that destroying the sheep and goats was necessary to bring the numbers in line with the carrying capacity of the land. Diné men and women responded that a better solution would be to expand the land base.
  - Nonetheless, beginning in 1933, the federal government initiated a decade-long program that reduced the Diné stock of goats and sheep by 50 percent. The experience proved traumatic to the Diné.

Nations That Adopted the IRA

- The tribal nations that adopted the IRA, in contrast, met mixed results. In Wisconsin, for example, the Stockbridge-Munsee used the new law to restore 15,000 acres of their former reservation, bolster self-government, and spark a period of political and economic renewal.

- ❖ Native tribes in the South experienced the IRA differently.
  - ❭ In North Carolina, the Lumbee, an unrecognized tribe located in Robeson County, responded eagerly to what they believed to be an opportunity to organize and gain federal acknowledgment through the new law.
  - ❭ However, after subjecting Lumbees to a variety of tests, the BIA rejected their effort to organize under the auspices of the IRA. The agency pointed to a lack of centralized political organization and "low blood quantum."

- ❖ The Mississippi Band of Choctaw Indians lived in similar circumstances, particularly in regard to their need to define a "third space" for their Indian identity in a biracial world that segregated black from white.
  - ❭ The Mississippi Band, which consisted of Choctaws who did not remove to the Indian Territory during the 1830s, secured some federal support from the BIA agency in 1918. But as a whole, they remained marginalized, poor, and politically powerless.
  - ❭ The IRA promised much-needed change. After the Choctaws voted to approve the IRA in 1934, some of them organized the Mississippi Choctaw Indian Federation and adopted a constitution.
  - ❭ At the same time, the local BIA agent took it upon himself to organize a separate representative body called the Tribal Business Committee. The debate that followed among the Mississippi Band was not about whether self-government was a good idea but on whose terms self-government would be exercised.
  - ❭ Despite their use of strikes, boycotts, and petitions, the Mississippi Choctaw Indian Federation lost out to what became the officially sanctioned tribal council in 1945—and then only after the Shell Oil Company wanted access to Choctaw oil.
  - ❭ However, over the course of the 20th century, members of the Mississippi Choctaw Indian Federation emerged as leaders on the tribal council, and the Indian New Deal served as the beginning of a remarkable renaissance.

- ❖ In the final analysis, the IRA provided a more compelling vision of the future than allotment and established, if imperfectly, the expectation

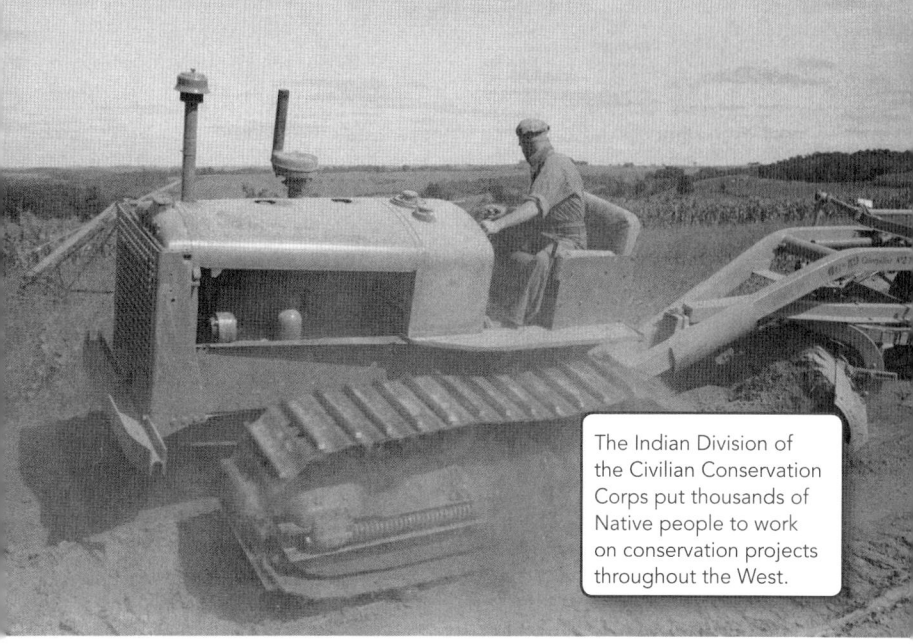

The Indian Division of the Civilian Conservation Corps put thousands of Native people to work on conservation projects throughout the West.

for self-government, land reconsolidation, and on-reservation economic development.

Other Dimensions of the Indian New Deal

❖ It's important to acknowledge that the Indian New Deal had many other dimensions than the IRA. The Indian Division of the Civilian Conservation Corps, for instance, provided direct relief by putting thousands of Native people to work.

❖ Meanwhile, the Works Progress Administration provided jobs building homes, renovating schools, and constructing roads, while also supporting American Indian writers and artists through the Federal Writers' Project and Federal Art Project.

❖ Finally, the Indian New Deal helped open the door to the protection of property rights based on aboriginal land claims and the acceptance of oral tradition as legitimate evidence in legal cases. This precedent was set in the Supreme Court case *United States v. Santa Fe Pacific Railroad Co.* in 1941.

Conclusions on the Indian New Deal

- Without the tenacity of Native people through the early 20th century and their persistent calls for reform, the Indian New Deal may not have happened at all.

- Adjusting our vision of the Great Depression and the New Deal allows us to see these hidden histories. We come to understand how, between the late 1920s and early 1940s, Native people set about making a New Deal for themselves and their communities during an era of uncertainty and convulsive change—one that was far from over as storm clouds gathered across Europe once more.

Suggested Reading

Ackley and Stanciu, eds., *Laura Cornelius Kellogg.*

Biolsi, *Organizing the Lakota.*

Deloria and Lytle, *The Nations Within.*

Maynor Lowery, *Lumbee Indians in the Jim Crow South.*

McMillan, *Making Indian Law.*

Questions to Consider

1. How did Native people contribute to the movement for reform that culminated in the Indian Reorganization Act of 1934?

2. What did the Indian Reorganization Act set out to do? What actually happened once it was implemented? Do you consider it a success or a failure? Why?

AMERICAN INDIANS AND WORLD WAR II

World War II and the onset of the atomic age powerfully shaped the lives of American Indians. Many hoped that the war would bring a "double victory" over fascism abroad and injustice at home. This lecture looks at the war's mixed legacies in Native America. We consider how it brought work opportunities but also displacement and internment. Meanwhile, the draft created a forum for debates over the meaning of citizenship. We then turn our attention to the thousands of American Indian men and women who served in the military. We conclude with case studies of Pima Marine Ira Hayes, nuclear energy development, and cultural revitalization to suggest that the double victory was unrealized by the end of the 1940s.

The Home Front

❖ By the late 1930s, overseas aggression increasingly drew the attention of President Franklin Delano Roosevelt and the American public away from the New Deal and the Depression. And, as early as 1939, some American Indians took symbolic action to help the nation present a unified front abroad despite cultural differences at home. For example, many Indians abandoned the swastika, although its traditional meaning was friendship, peace, and good luck.

❖ When the Japanese attacked Pearl Harbor on December 7, 1941, the United States assumed a war footing. On the home front, the response of Native peoples to the war was diverse. In some areas, a wave of patriotism washed over communities. During the war, American Indians demonstrated support by purchasing about $50 million in war bonds and planting "victory gardens" to keep the cost of food down, which saved the military money to supply troops overseas.

- ❖ The Bureau of Indian Affairs (BIA) also negotiated leases that allowed for the exploitation of tribal agricultural and grazing lands, timber stands, and subsurface minerals, such as oil, coal, gas, and manganese. Unfortunately, the BIA frequently approved these leases without first securing tribal consent, and the profits often benefited the non-Indians to whom Native land had been leased at below market value.

- ❖ The practice of leasing tribal land in the name of patriotic duty also brought Japanese internment to Native America. In February 1942, Roosevelt signed an executive order that empowered the U.S. government to force about 120,000 Japanese and Japanese Americans living on the West Coast to reside in 10 major internment centers for the duration of the war.
  - › Never one to miss an opportunity, Indian Commissioner John Collier reached out to the newly formed War Relocation Authority—which administered the centers—and volunteered to lease tribal lands for Japanese internment. Two internment centers were established.
  - › Though Collier expected that the tribes would benefit from internal improvements—such as road construction, the cultivation of agricultural lands, and the development of dormitories and barracks—they did not.

Native Interment

- ❖ Native communities not only received displaced peoples in internment camps, but they were also forced to live in internment camps.

- ❖ This is precisely what happened after the Japanese invaded the Pribilof and the Aleutian Islands in June 1942. The Japanese occupied Attu Island, taking 42 Aleuts prisoner—only half of whom lived to see their release.

- ❖ The United States, citing military necessity, swiftly forced approximately 900 Aleuts living west of Unimak Island from their homes and into dilapidated dormitories at abandoned fish canneries and mines in remote areas of southeastern Alaska. There, they lived in squalor, without adequate food, heat, or shelter and in the absence of medical care.

- In May 1944, the survivors of the camps returned to find that their personal and community property had been looted, vandalized, and destroyed and that military equipment and hazardous debris remained strewn about the islands. It would take more than four decades to receive compensation and begin the restoration.

Struggle over Civil Rights

- In Alaska's mainland towns and cities, the war prompted another kind of struggle—one over civil rights.

- Elizabeth and Roy Peratrovich, a Tlingit couple with leadership roles in the Alaska Native Brotherhood and Alaska Native Sisterhood, fought for basic citizenship rights and against acts of discrimination and segregation that were routinely directed toward Alaska Natives.
    - In March 1944, the efforts of the Alaska Native Brotherhood and Alaska Native Sisterhood were bolstered by an Inupiat teenager named Alberta Schenck, who was arrested for refusing to leave the "whites-only" section of a movie theater in Nome.
    - The Peratroviches' letters and Schenck's detention captured the attention of Alaska Governor Ernest Gruening. His support led the territorial legislature to adopt an Anti-Discrimination Act in February 1945.

- Lakota allottees on the Pine Ridge Reservation were not as successful. In August 1942, the U.S. government seized more than 300,000 acres in the northwest corner of the reservation for an Air Force aerial gunnery and bombing range. More than 100 Lakotas were given less than two weeks to leave their homes, and many ended up in tents and slum areas of neighboring towns and cities.

Pan-Tribal Organization Efforts

- In addition to contributing to political mobilization at the tribal level, the war also accelerated pan-tribal organization efforts.

- In November 1944, for instance, 80 delegates from 50 tribes and associations in 27 states met to establish an organization called the National Congress of American Indians (NCAI). The NCAI envisioned itself as a tribal "united nations" that would provide a way for Indians to express their shared concerns with one voice.

- In keeping with the notion of a double victory, the NCAI's initial platform called for Native inclusion in the G.I. Bill, the guarantee of voting rights in state elections, and an end to legal and de facto segregation.

- The NCAI also emphasized respect for tribal sovereignty, cultural pluralism, and treaty rights. The organization included in its initial resolutions a call for an Indian Claims Commission to provide restitution for treaty violations and other outstanding claims against the federal government.

Cultural Revitalization

- Along with political activism came cultural revitalization in the form of warrior societies, dances, songs, and ceremonies. For example, in the Pacific Northwest, Makah fathers danced in traditional masks and regalia to celebrate the return of their sons from World War II.

- After the war, Gus Palmer Sr., a Kiowa veteran who flew in 21 bombing missions, spearheaded the revitalization of the Kiowa Black Leggings Warrior Society in honor of his brother, Lyndreth Palmer, who was killed in France, as well as all other Kiowa veterans.

- Elsewhere, American Indian people were leaving reservation homes to seek opportunities in airplane factories, ordnance depots, shipyards, railroads, gold and copper mines, sawmills, and canneries in large cities across the country. Indeed, about 40,000 American Indians sought opportunities in the war industries, including an estimated 12,000 women by 1943.

The Selective Training and Service Act

- If some Native people responded to the onset of war with patriotic demonstrations of U.S. citizenship, others looked on it as an opportunity to underscore the primacy they placed on their indigenous national identities.

- By 1924, universal citizenship had been extended to American Indians, but many did not want it. Thus, when the Selective Training and Service Act was passed in September 1940, some citizens of tribal nations challenged its legitimacy.

- The Haudenosaunee or Iroquois Confederacy—always at the forefront of the sovereignty struggle—took the United States to court over the draft. In October 1940, citing the 18th-century Treaty of Canandaigua, the confederacy contended that the United States did not have the authority to impose U.S. citizenship.

- The Second Circuit Court of Appeals ruled against the Haudenosaunee in November 1941, but it did provide an opportunity to assert sovereignty. John Collier and the Haudenosaunee staged a public event at which the Haudenosaunee declared war on the Axis powers independently and pledged to defeat the Axis powers as an ally to the United States.

- Despite such acts of resistance, by war's end, about 44,000 Native Americans had served in the U.S. armed forces during the conflict as fighter pilots, gunners, bombardiers, and other such roles. Meanwhile, approximately 800 Native women enlisted in auxiliary branches, such as the Women's Army Corps and the Navy's Women Accepted for Volunteer Emergency Services.

- The American Indians who ultimately emerged most visibly from the war were the Navajo code talkers. In the spring of 1942, 29 Navajo men were recruited to devise a way to send and receive coded messages during combat. In time, the code expanded, and 400 Navajos would join the code talkers. The code proved central to the Pacific campaign in a variety of contexts, including underwater demolition and air reconnaissance.

The Manhattan Project

- From the Manhattan Project forward, the atomic age that was inaugurated by the war had everything to do with Native America, and it is difficult to find a victory for Native people in it. For instance, for the Navajo and Lakota, the end of World War II and the beginning of the atomic age brought underground and open-pit uranium mining, chronic health problems for those who worked in them, and ongoing environmental concerns in the areas surrounding them.

- The life of Ira Hayes, an Akimel O'odham man from the Gila River Reservation in Arizona, provides another penetrating answer to the question of whether the war achieved a double victory.
    - Hayes was born in 1923 and raised on the Gila River Reservation. As a young man, he worked in the Indian Division of the New Deal's Civilian Conservation Corps. He enlisted in the Marines in August 1942, at the age of 19. And in February 1945, he took part in the assault on Iwo Jima.
    - The difficulty that Hayes faced upon his return home and his attempted adjustment to civilian life suggests how far short Native American service members fell of attaining that double victory after World War II.
    - During the early 1950s, Hayes attempted to take advantage of the BIA's "voluntary relocation program," which purported to give Indians the chance to find better jobs and standards of living and to promote assimilation by encouraging them to move from their reservation homes to major cities.
    - Hayes struggled with alcoholism, and he learned that support for relocation was inadequate. After bouncing around and returning home only to leave again, he ended up back on the Gila River Reservation, picking cotton.

Ira Hayes was one of the soldiers captured in the iconic sculpture photograph of the flag raising at the top of Mount Suribachi, after it was seized on February 23.

- > It was there that he died one January night in 1955. He was found outside near his home; the cause of death was deemed exposure and alcohol poisoning.
- > Not long after Hayes's passing, folksinger Peter La Farge wrote these potent words in regard to the tragic end of his life: "Call him drunken Ira Hayes. He won't answer anymore. Not the whiskey-drinking Indian or the Marine who went to war."

❖ World War II and the world it made transformed the lives of American Indian men and women, and it forever altered the demographic, political, cultural, and physical landscapes of Native America. Instead of a double victory, it brought an uncertain one.

Suggested Reading

Bernstein, *American Indians and World War II*.

Ellis, *A Dancing People*.

Kohlhoff, *When the Wind Was a River*.

Nez and Avila, *Code Talker*.

Rosier, *Serving Their Country*.

Questions to Consider

1. In what ways do you see Native experiences during World War II as being the same as those of other Americans? What made them distinctive?
2. How do you account for the mixed legacy of this era in Indian Country? In what ways did it realize the promise of the double victory? In what ways did it fall short? How do you account for this?

INDIAN TERMINATION OR SELF-DETERMINATION?

Lecture 22

The advent of a new threat to tribal sovereignty in the form of the federal government's termination policy contributed to a multifaceted rights movement that gained momentum by the end of the 1960s. At the heart of the contest were two visions of freedom and what it might mean: sameness or sovereignty. In this lecture, we begin by exploring the debate over termination. Then we turn our attention to the American Indian youth movement, the fishing-rights struggle in the Pacific Northwest, and the intersection of the Native rights struggle with the Civil Rights Movement, War on Poverty, Vietnam, and global decolonization.

Termination

- ❖ Termination was a federal government policy intended to eliminate all federal obligations to tribal nations. Through termination, reservations would become counties. Tribal governments would become municipalities. And the responsibility to provide services, as well as criminal and civil jurisdiction, would be transferred to the states. Treaties would become dead letters, rather than living documents that acknowledged inherent sovereignty.

- ❖ Termination, in other words, envisioned a "citizenship of sameness." Those in favor of it wanted the only nation Native people to claim as their own to be the United States.

- ❖ Senator Arthur V. Watkins, a Republican from Utah, saw termination as a "freedom program," but of course, it had nothing to do with freedom. In reality, it was about intolerance toward cultural pluralism, a desire for access to tribal lands and resources, the reduction of federal expenditures, and the abolition of treaty rights and tribal sovereignty.

- Termination's vision of civil rights and equality, then, amounted to ending the federal government's trust relationship with tribal nations.

- During the 1940s and 1950s, proponents of termination began to put their plan into action. Ironically, one of the most effective tools was the Indian Claims Commission (ICC), something tribal rights advocates had been demanding for decades.
    - Established in 1946, the ICC created a forum in which tribes could bring forward claims associated with treaty violations—including the illegal taking and undervaluing of land and resources—and secure compensation for them.
    - But terminationists put the ICC to an entirely different purpose, using successful claims as leverage. For instance, Watkins would draft legislation that required tribes to terminate their relationship with the federal government simply to receive the claims they had justly won in the ICC!

- Termination also gained momentum with the appointment of Dillon S. Myer as Truman's commissioner of Indian affairs from 1950 to 1953. In addition to working against economic development on reservations, Myer wanted state governments to assume responsibility for tribal health, education, and welfare programs. He also expanded the voluntary relocation program, which provided federal incentives for Natives to move to urban areas.

170 Native Peoples of North America

Putting the Policies into Action

- If the ICC and relocation gave termination momentum, House Concurrent Resolution 108 and Public Law 280, both of which were adopted in August 1953, put the dreaded policies into action.
  - For example, HCR 108 stated that it was the "sense of Congress" that all tribes in California, Florida, New York, Texas, and other areas, should be "freed from Federal supervision and control and from all disabilities and limitations specially applicable to Indians."
  - Here was freedom rendered as the "citizenship of sameness."

- Two weeks later, Congress passed Public Law 280, which provided for the extension of state civil and criminal jurisdiction over tribes in a number of states—without even having to secure tribal consent. The law also opened the door for other states to take similar action. In the following session of Congress, 12 termination bills were presented.

Self-Determination

- Native rights organizations, such as the NCAI, countered the termination movement by advancing a different vision of freedom, one we can think of as self-determination. This vision included all the rights accorded to U.S. citizens, but it also distinguished tribal nations from other racial and ethnic minority groups. As citizens of tribal nations, Native people also insisted on the continued acknowledgment of treaty rights, tribal lands, and self-government.

- As hearings on the termination bills began in February 1954, the NCAI issued a formal Declaration of Indian Rights.
  - This document flatly rejected the notion that termination gave Native people anything. As sovereign equals, argued the NCAI, tribes had accepted "Federal protection and the promise of certain benefits" in return for "title to the very soil of our beloved country." Further, reservations were not "places of confinement" but "ancestral homelands. … We feel we must assert our right to maintain ownership in our own way, and to terminate it only by our consent."

- > The NCAI didn't reject the ultimate goal of attaining greater political and economic autonomy from the Bureau of Indian Affairs (BIA). Instead, the organization clarified that autonomy could not come at the expense of the nation-to-nation treaty relationships tribes had forged with the United States.
  - > If termination of federal services were to proceed, it would have to be done gradually, only after full consultation and consent and with no bearing on tribes' legal status as sovereign nations.

- ❖ Among the people most responsible for articulating this alternative vision of freedom was activist D'Arcy McNickle.
  - > In 1944, McNickle helped to found the NCAI and, there, became convinced that the U.S. approach to international development offered a better model for federal-Indian relations.
  - > McNickle eventually drafted an approach to self-determination that took inspiration from the Point Four Program. This program was an approach to international development in which the United States would provide training and technical assistance to developing nations.
  - > The goal of Point Four was not to control these governments but to equip them with the resources they needed to modernize. The NCAI adopted McNickle's idea and lobbied Congress to replace HCR 108 with it.

The American Indian Youth Movement

- ❖ In the late 1950s and early 1960s, the American Indian youth movement grew out of an influx of Native people on college and university campuses following World War II.

- ❖ The politicization of these students largely took place at the Workshops on American Indian Affairs. Over time, the workshops came to serve as an intellectual training ground for young people. Eventually, they would put forward yet another definition of freedom through an organization of their own, the National Indian Youth Council (NIYC).

- The incipient youth movement intersected with and was transformed by the American Indian Chicago Conference in June 1961. The conference brought together hundreds of tribal representatives from across Indian Country to draft a Declaration of Indian Purpose to be delivered to President John F. Kennedy.

- Students attending that year's Workshops on American Indian Affairs participated in the conferred. But some of them, including Clyde Warrior, Mel Thom, Bruce Wilkie, and Shirley Hill Witt, formed their own caucus and advocated for more strident demands and harsher critiques of the federal government.

- In succeeding years, the Workshops on American Indian Affairs became both a meeting place and an intellectual training ground for the youth movement. Cherokee anthropologist Robert K. Thomas seized on the opportunity to train a generation of young people to lead a nationalistic pan-Indian movement.

Fishing-Rights Movement

- In late 1963 and early 1964, the NIYC's activism intersected with a grassroots fishing-rights movement along the Nisqually and Puyallup Rivers in the Pacific Northwest.

- For decades, the state of Washington had been harassing Native people for exercising their "reserved rights" to hunt and fish in "usual and accustomed places." The crisis escalated after the passage of Public Law 280, as the state, citing concerns over conservation, started closing the rivers, arresting Indian fishers, and confiscating their equipment.

- Activist Billy Frank, a former Marine, lived along the Nisqually. He was joined by all manner of fishing-rights activists and advocates, including actor Marlon Brando, comedian Dick Gregory, Canadian Cree folk singer Buffy Sainte-Marie, and such critically important figures as Janet McCloud, a Tulalip, and Hank Adams, an Assiniboine.

Vine Deloria Jr.

- By 1964, Vine Deloria Jr. became the executive director of the NCAI and quickly breathed new life into the organization. He used editorials in the organization's newsletter, testimony in Congress, annual meetings, and interactions with federal officials to blunt termination and promote tribal self-determination.

- In one of Deloria's most important victories, he orchestrated the effort to defeat the Indian Resources Development Act, legislation that Interior Secretary Stewart Udall promised would revolutionize Indian Country but drafted without tribal consultation.

- In the spring of 1968 major breakthroughs appeared imminent. The War on Poverty, with its emphasis on "maximum feasible participation" and "local initiative" had become a critically important source of leverage against the paternalism of the BIA.

- Termination had all but stopped, but it had already taken a terrible toll on the 100 tribes, bands, and rancherias (dwelling places of rancheros) subjected to it. Moreover, the Pacific Northwest fishing-rights campaign was being thwarted by lower-court decisions, the War on Poverty was being underfunded, racial tensions were intensifying, and the war in Vietnam was beginning to look ever more like an act of American imperialism.

Poor People's Campaign

- The Poor People's Campaign was a six-week protest held in 1968 in Washington DC. In the spring of that year, thousands of poor whites, blacks, Latinos, and American Indians converged on the capital, taking up residence in Resurrection City, a shantytown constructed along West Potomac Park, and in churches and schools throughout the city.

- Together, they marched, testified before Congress, conducted sit-ins, and allowed themselves to be arrested—all in an effort to expose what they considered to be the grave injustices visited on the poor. Among the protests was a spontaneous sit-in at BIA headquarters.

The Poor People's Campaign was the last great vision of civil rights leader Martin Luther King Jr.

- The NCAI acknowledged what brought the Poor People's Campaign to Washington, but it did not endorse American Indian participation—in part because it feared treaty rights would be lost in the mix and in part because it did not approve of the tactics. Such activists as Mel Thom, Tillie Walker, Hank Adams, and Bob Dumont, along with dozens of other Native people from communities across Indian Country disagreed. Thom asserted, "There is no way to improve upon racism, immorality and colonialism; it can only be done away with."

- By locating their struggle in the context of decolonization, the Indian delegation demanded a third image of freedom—one that envisioned not only self-determination but national liberation.

- The Poor People's Campaign continued into the third week of June. It was the indecisive end of a pivotally important era in American Indian history. From the late 1940s to the late 1960s, two visions of freedom came into conflict with each other: termination and self-determination. Out of that conflict was born yet another vision that called not only for self-determination but national liberation.

Suggested Reading

Castile, *To Show Heart*.

Cobb, *Native Activism in Cold War America*.

Cowger, *The National Congress of American Indians*.

Fixico, *Termination and Relocation*.

Shreve, *Red Power Rising*.

Questions to Consider

1. What were the major components of the termination policy, and how did they work to realize a vision of freedom that replaced sovereignty with sameness? How did American Indian activists counter that vision?

2. What were the ideas at the heart of the Workshops on American Indian Affairs, the fishing-rights struggle, and the Poor People's Campaign? How did they evoke a different meaning of freedom in Indian Country?

NATIVE RADICALISM AND REFORM, 1969–1978

Lecture 23

The late 1960s and 1970s witnessed a spike in Indian direct action through the occupation of Alcatraz Island, the Trail of Broken Treaties, Wounded Knee II, and the Longest Walk. Throughout the period, as Standing Rock Sioux intellectual Vine Deloria Jr. noted, there was a tension between "being militant" and being "nationalistic." This lecture considers how Native activists attempted to strike a balance between them. It also explores other sites of politically purposeful action, including Congress and the courts.

Alcatraz

- ❖ The 19-month occupation of Alcatraz Island in San Francisco Bay began on November 20, 1969. The idea for the occupation grew out of the concerns of the San Francisco Indian community, particularly after the local Indian center burned down.
  - › It was also meant to address the concerns of Native faculty and students from UCLA, Berkeley; Santa Cruz; Chico; and San Francisco State, who wanted to use the occupation to address their concerns over the paucity of courses, programs, and services focused specifically on American Indians.
  - › But Alcatraz quickly became a symbol of indigenous survival in North America and, indeed, throughout the Western Hemisphere, despite centuries of colonialism.

- ❖ Calling themselves the Indians of All Tribes, the 78 mostly college-aged young people who launched the occupation of Alcatraz were led by Richard Oakes, a charismatic Mohawk from the St. Regis Reservation. The media immediately descended on Alcatraz, and the Indians of All Tribes garnered what seemed to be universal support.

- The occupiers explained that they had seized the island because it was abandoned federal property and that, according to an article of the 1868 Fort Laramie Treaty, they had the right to demand that the federal government return it to American Indian ownership.

- But Oakes highlighted the even greater significance of their actions when he said, "This is actually a move, not so much to liberate the island, but to liberate ourselves." The occupation of Alcatraz was about decolonization.

- The Indians of All Tribes then issued a formal proclamation explaining why the island prison made a perfect place to launch their liberation movement. Alcatraz had much in common with reservations, they argued. It was isolated and had no fresh running water. Unemployment was high, there were no health care facilities, and its residents, like so many Native people living on reservations, were reduced to abject dependency.

- The Indians of All Tribes also identified concrete actions to restore the island and revitalize tribal communities, including the establishment of a

Alcatraz Island

Center for Native American Studies, a spiritual center, and an American Indian Center of Ecology. Two more proposals called for the creation of a Great Indian Training School and an American Indian Museum.

❖ The occupation is widely remembered as a time of unity, shared purpose, and freedom. But it also brought hardship and tragedy. In January 1970, Oakes's young daughter fell to her death. Six months later, a massive fire swept across the island, and yet another incident left coordinator LaNada Means with severe burns. Further, drugs, alcohol, and violence became increasingly hard to control.

❖ Meanwhile, the Nixon administration attempted to blunt the protestors' efforts. The federal government offered to turn Alcatraz over to the National Park Service and include monuments to Indians, but the occupiers rejected the proposal as patronizing.

❖ Eventually, public interest and support flagged. In time, the government cut off power and telephone service to the island, making conditions virtually unlivable. When the dozen or so people who remained on "the Rock" were quietly evicted on June 11, 1971, it was almost as if the occupation had never happened.

❖ Yet, as a symbol of political liberation and cultural survival, Alcatraz lived on. The activism there sparked occupations of abandoned federal property and government buildings—as many as 74 of them—elsewhere.

The Trail of Broken Treaties

❖ As the occupation of Alcatraz wound down, another organization, the American Indian Movement (AIM) came to the fore. Founded in July 1968, AIM initially focused on urban issues, including access to social services and adequate housing, racism, and police brutality. The scope of its activism, however, expanded swiftly. One of its most crucial undertakings was the Trail of Broken Treaties.

- The Trail of Broken Treaties began in October 1972; caravans of protestors bound for Washington DC left Seattle, San Francisco, and Los Angeles. By the time the three caravans converged in St. Paul, Minnesota, they were 600 strong.

- There, Hank Adams, a former NIYC member who was central to the Pacific Northwest fishing-rights struggle, helped draft a set of demands the group intended to present to Nixon, just in time for that November's national elections.

- The Twenty Points, as these demands were called, offered what has been described as "a new paradigm of dealing with Indian nations." Among other things, the Twenty Points demanded:
    - The restoration of treaty making, which Congress had ended in 1871
    - An annual summit in which Native leaders addressed Congress
    - The return of the 110 million acres of land that had been lost since the allotment era
    - The restoration of terminated tribes and the repeal of state jurisdiction
    - The establishment of a new office of federal-Indian relations.

- The Trail of Broken Treaties, however, didn't go as planned.
    - The protestors arrived just a week before the national elections, and the capital was a veritable ghost town. Most members of Congress were campaigning in their home states.
    - To make matters worse, no logistical arrangements had been made. This led to the snap decision to go the Bureau of Indian Affairs (BIA) building, located just blocks from the White House. Soon, about 1,000 Native people packed the BIA auditorium, while others worked with federal officials to find other accommodations.
    - When riot police unexpectedly showed up, protestors prepared for a siege. To underscore the sovereign status of tribal nations, they unfurled a banner that read "Native American Embassy" for everyone on the outside to see.
    - The tense, unplanned occupation of the BIA building lasted from November 3 to November 9, when a federal court affirmed the right

of the government to evict the protesters if they did not leave on their own. As soon as that news hit, the protestors ransacked the building.

- In the weeks that followed, the Twenty Points went unaddressed by the Nixon administration, and the media seemed more concerned about damage visited on the building than what the building represented to Native people.

Wounded Knee II

- The 71-day occupation of Wounded Knee on the Pine Ridge Reservation in South Dakota followed very shortly in the wake of the Trail of Broken Treaties.

- The trouble started after a man named Richard "Dickie" Wilson was elected tribal chairman of the Oglala Sioux at Pine Ridge, by a narrow margin, in 1972. He took the reins of a government that was already considered unrepresentative by many traditional Lakota. To make matters worse, Wilson had taken unpopular stances on two important issues involving tribal lands and was also charged with nepotism and corruption.

- When Lakotas began pressing for impeachment hearings, Wilson responded by assembling a private militia called the Guardians of the Oglala Nation (GOONs) to intimidate and harass his detractors.

- The impeachment initiative failed in February 1973. Fearing retaliation, Wilson's opponents invited AIM to Pine Ridge to protect them. Meetings between community members and AIM ended with a decision to take action.

- On February 27, 1973, about 200 people occupied the hamlet of Wounded Knee, the site of the devastating massacre of hundreds of Lakota by the United States cavalry in December 1890. After an early compromise fell apart, the activists proclaimed the establishment of the Independent Oglala Nation.

- ❖ The federal government's response was almost unbelievable. Federal marshals, FBI agents, and Wilson's GOONs surrounded the hamlet. They were armed with .50-caliber machine guns and M16 rifles and were supported by 17 armored personnel carriers and Phantom jets.

- ❖ The occupation ended on May 8, 1973—after 71 tense days, hours of negotiations, and the deaths of two Native men.

- ❖ Like Alcatraz and the Trail of Broken Treaties, there wasn't a clear resolution. Wilson not only remained in power but also inaugurated a "reign of terror" that contributed to unprecedented levels of violence at Pine Ridge. At the same time, legal proceedings, internal discord, and FBI infiltration crippled AIM.

- ❖ And yet, as with Alcatraz and the Trail of Broken Treaties, the Wounded Knee occupation symbolized a new beginning for the sovereignty movement for many American Indians.

- ❖ In addition, the media coverage these events generated—together with the publication of Vine Deloria Jr.'s *Custer Died for Your Sins* in 1969, as well as other books—helped make non–Native Americans more aware of and perhaps sympathetic to Indian rights.

- That sympathy, in turn, likely contributed to increased federal action through Congress and the courts that bolstered long-standing tribal demands for self-determination.

- In addition to militancy, activism took other forms during the late 1960s and 1970s, including literature, music, art, education, and international law. The struggle for restoration—a movement taken up by all of the tribes that were terminated during the 1950s and 1960s—was one of the most efficacious forms that sought change through Congressional action. Both Congress and the courts proved to be uncertain allies.

The Longest Walk

- The Longest Walk, an event also spearheaded by the AIM, played a significant role in propelling this effort forward, as well.

- It followed on the heels of the International NGO Conference on Discrimination against Indigenous Populations in the Americas, which convened at the United Nations' offices in Geneva, Switzerland, in September 1977.

- The Longest Walk began with a ceremony on Alcatraz Island in February 1978. Participants then made a 3,200-mile march to Washington DC, arriving on July 15, 1978.

- At the heart of the Longest Walk were several ideas: sovereignty and treaty rights, the continued validity of traditional knowledge and teachings, an indigenous environmental ethic, ongoing concerns for the rights of indigenous women, the need for a final reckoning with settler colonialism, and the solidarity of the Western Hemisphere's indigenous peoples.

- Like the occupation of Alcatraz, the Trail of Broken Treaties, and Wounded Knee, the significance of the Longest Walk resides primarily in what it conveyed symbolically about the survival of Native nations, of tribal values and cultures, and of sovereignty and peoplehood. But this does not diminish their efficacy.

- Taken together, all of these forms of activism during the late 1960s and through the 1970s suggest that Vine Deloria Jr.'s distinction between militancy and nationalism may not be so easily drawn.

- Radicals and reformers, artists and musicians, educators and organizers from the grassroots to the global had all done their part to raise American Indians to a new conception of themselves and to push Congress, the courts, and several presidential administrations to do the same. Having reestablished a foothold for tribal sovereignty, focus turned to testing its limits.

Suggested Reading

Davis, *Survival Schools.*

Deloria, *Custer Died for Your Sins.*

Johnson, Nagel, and Champagne, eds., *American Indian Activism.*

Sims, *Fritz Scholder.*

Smith and Warrior, *Like a Hurricane.*

Questions to Consider

1. Do you think that the activism highlighted in this lecture suggests that Native activists met the challenge posed by Vine Deloria Jr. to go beyond "making wild threats and militant statements" and, in so doing, "raise an entire group to a new conception of themselves"?

2. What other forms did politically purposeful action take during the late 1960s and 1970s? Why do we typically not think about these "nonmilitant" ways in which Native people have engaged in activism?

REASSERTING RIGHTS AND TRIBAL SOVEREIGNTY

Lecture 24

Since the late 1970s, American Indians have not only survived seemingly insurmountable odds, but have aggressively tested the limits of individual rights and tribal sovereignty. This lecture explores a few of the many critical sites of contemporary sovereignty struggles, including gaming, repatriation, religious freedom, recognition, self-governance, jurisdiction, and resource development. We find that the terrain over which sovereignty's limits are tested is vast and that the ground is both uneven and shifting.

Gaming

* Gaming has been the single most successful means of promoting economic development in reservation communities since it took off in the late 1980s.

* Indeed, prior to gaming, economic development strategies were largely dictated by the federal government, geared more toward enriching non-Native individuals and corporations than tribal people and were often exploitative of Native rights and resources.

* Poverty and unemployment were, and in many places still are, rampant, and tribal governments typically could not afford to provide services to their citizens. Because of this, reservations were dependent on a "transfer economy," meaning they relied on funds coming from the federal government or other public assistance programs rather than generating revenue from private or tribally owned enterprises.

* The Florida Seminole brought gaming to the fore when they opened a high-stakes bingo operation on their Hollywood Reservation between

Fort Lauderdale and Miami in 1979. By the mid-1980s, 120 other tribes had followed suit.

- State governments reacted defensively. Florida and California, for instance, insisted on the right of states to regulate tribal gaming, and their actions sent the matter to the Supreme Court. The concept of tribal sovereignty emerged victorious in *California v. Cabazon Band of Mission Indians* in 1987. In a 6 to 3 decision, the justices found that if tribal gaming were going to be regulated, only the federal government could do it.

- Congress then promptly set out to do exactly that with passage of the Indian Gaming Regulatory Act of 1988. The legislation recognized the right of tribal governments to engage in gaming on trust land as an exercise of tribal sovereignty, while simultaneously limiting it.

- Following the legislation, tribal economies experienced explosive growth. The total annual revenue generated by gaming rocketed from $5.4 billion in 1995 to $26.5 billion in 2009—a fivefold increase in less than 15 years. The gains have increased, if more slowly, ever since.

- All across the United States, tribes contributed to the employment of Indians and non-Indians, invested in the infrastructure of surrounding communities, and helped revitalize depressed economies.

- Unfortunately, public misperceptions of gaming, the overemphasis on conflict between tribes and states, and the media's tendency to portray tribes as "getting rich quick" mask the reality of the important work gaming revenue does within and beyond tribal communities.

- It's important to note, too, that the billions of dollars generated annually by Indian gaming do not get distributed evenly across Indian Country, nor has the much-needed revenue alleviated the dire state of many reservation economies.

Repatriation

- Basically, from the very beginning of the colonial encounter, non-Native people have been looting battlefields and massacre sites and robbing Indian graves. These macabre activities have included the taking of everything from sacred objects to human remains, and they contributed to museum collections across the United States and beyond.

- These institutions, of course, saw themselves as doing "good work" by "preserving vanishing cultures" and were certainly not counting on Native people being around to have a problem with their collecting practices. But, of course, things didn't work out that way.

- After many long years of protest and political action, Congress passed the Native American Graves Protection and Repatriation Act in 1990.

- This legislation required federal agencies and other institutions that received federal money, such as museums, to account for the human remains, funerary and sacred objects, and objects of cultural patrimony in their collections. Then they had to give tribes an opportunity to reclaim the items within repatriatable categories that could be "culturally identified" as belonging to them.

- The act has served to strengthen communication and collaboration between tribes and museums and has brought about new kinds of museum work on many levels.

Religious Freedom

- Peyote is a spineless cactus that, when ingested, has hallucinogenic properties. By the early 20th century, the peyote religion, also known as the Peyote Way, had spread from Mexico through Texas and Oklahoma and then all across the West. In 1918, the Native American Church incorporated, in part to give the peyote religion protection under U.S. laws.

- All the while, state and federal lawmakers attempted to pass legislation to regulate the use, possession, and transportation of peyote. This trend culminated in peyote being included in the Controlled Substances Act of 1970. The Native American Church was supposed to be exempted, but this did not prevent authorities from harassing Native people, and they were still subjected to prosecution.

- In 1978, Congress enacted the American Indian Religious Freedom Act (AIRFA) to "protect and preserve for American Indians their inherent right of freedom to believe, express, and exercise ... traditional religions." But did the act protect the sacramental use of peyote?

- That question was at the heart of *Oregon v. Smith*, a pivotal Supreme Court case decided in 1990. In a stinging defeat for free exercise of religion, the court ruled that the state of Oregon could fire and refuse unemployment compensation to two Native men for failing a drug test due to their religious use of peyote.

- Reuben Snake, a Ho-Chunk leader in the Native American Church, emerged as one of the most articulate defenders of the Peyote Way in the wake of *Oregon v. Smith*. He proved instrumental in pushing Congress to amend AIRFA in 1994 so that it specifically protected the sacramental use of peyote.

- While passage of the 1994 amendment turned out to be a victory for the free exercise of religion, it also underscored how unreliable the federal system had become—and remains—when it comes to the limits of religious freedom.

Recognition

- The issue of federal recognition or acknowledgment, perhaps more than any other, gets to the heart of the federal government's ability to limit sovereignty, because it revolves around who gets to decide who is or is not considered legally "Indian."

- Tribal nations that engaged in treaty making with the United States established clear political and legal relationships. And, in so doing, their status as nations was recognized by the United States. But many tribal communities, particularly those in the East, did not enter into treaties with the United States. And still others, such as California tribes, entered into treaties only to have the U.S. Senate fail to ratify them.

- Federal acknowledgment of tribal status is important because it establishes a trust relationship with the U.S. government. And that trust relationship entitles tribal nations to federal funding and services, including health, welfare, and education, as well as training and technical assistance. Moreover, it makes it possible for tribes to take land into trust, to be self-governing, to engage in economic development, and to establish and enforce their own laws.

- During the late 1970s, the Bureau of Indian Affairs (BIA) created the Office of Federal Acknowledgment and a set of criteria for tribal communities seeking federal recognition. The criteria, however, proved to be so restrictive and burdensome that very few of the tribes seeking acknowledgment could meet them.

- At the same time, local and state officials opposed acknowledgment because they didn't want land to be removed from tax rolls, something that happens when land is brought into trust by the federal government.

- Underlying questions of authenticity were at play, too, as critics of tribes seeking acknowledgment questioned whether the petitioners were "really Indians."

- Federal acknowledgment demonstrates how much power people outside tribal communities have in deciding who can lay claim to the political-legal identity of being Indian. And, in so doing, they effectively limit (and even prevent) tribes from exercising sovereignty.

Self-Governance

- During the 1990s, Congress expanded the capacity of tribal governments to exercise self-determination by passing legislation that put into place something called compacting.

- Compacts are essentially block grants funded by category, such as housing, education, and law enforcement. They're intended to diminish federal control over the management of tribal affairs while allowing the government to continue to acknowledge its trust obligations to tribes.

- As of 2015, more than 300 Native nations had compacts for BIA and Indian Health Service programs that were worth about $2 billion.

Jurisdiction

- Contests over legal jurisdiction have become critical sites for negotiations over the limits of tribal sovereignty. In fact, there have been many battles, including the power of tribes to tax non-Indian corporations and individuals and the power of tribal courts (in accordance with the Indian

Child Welfare Act) to determine the fate of children who have been put up for adoption.

❖ Another important site of contestation involves civil and criminal jurisdiction, as Congress and the courts negotiate where federal, state, and tribal laws begin and end in the context of everything from misdemeanors to murder.

❖ Making matters more complex, jurisdiction shifts if the situation involves only Indians, only non-Indians, or both and whether the crimes occur on trust land.

Resource Development

❖ By the 1990s and early 2000s, heightened concerns over sustainability and climate change contributed to a push for different forms of economic development, such as solar, wind, and other renewables.

❖ Through organizations such as the Indian Country Renewable Energy Consortium and the Intertribal Council on Utility Policy—and with the support of federal legislation and innovative partnerships with states—tribal governments and organizations have made strides in resource management and the production of clean energy.

❖ Indigenous people have also taken to the streets, as evidenced by the massive People's Climate March held in New York City in advance of a United Nations climate summit in late 2014.

❖ Despite these promising signs, the struggle over the Keystone XL pipeline suggests that battles over resource development and sovereignty are far from over. The Keystone pipeline—a vast system that carries oil from Alberta, Canada, through the Dakotas and Nebraska and then branches into Illinois and Texas—traverses nearly 3,000 miles.

❖ Keystone XL, a proposed expansion, would add another many more miles to the system and cut diagonally from Alberta, through the

- Bakken region in Montana, and end in Steele City, Nebraska. In getting there, the pipeline would cut through environmentally sensitive areas, including the vital Ogallala Aquifer.

- Between 2010 and 2015, First Nations and American Indian activists allied to protest Keystone XL on a number of grounds, including carbon dioxide emissions and the disruption of sacred and ancestral sites.

- When U.S. President Barack Obama vetoed a bill that would have approved construction of Keystone XL in February 2015 and then rejected TransCanada's application to build the pipeline in November of that year, the alliance read it as a significant, if tentative, victory for tribal sovereignty.

Suggested Reading

Cattelino, *High Stakes*.

Miller, *Forgotten Tribes*.

Thomas, *Skull Wars*.

Wilkinson, *Blood Struggle*.

Williams, *Like a Loaded Weapon*.

Questions to Consider

1. In what specific ways have American Indians tested the limits of individual rights and tribal sovereignty since the late 1970s?

2. What accounts for the uneven and shifting ground on which these ongoing assertions of individual rights sovereignty and survival take place? In other words, why are assertions of individual rights and sovereignty often met with resistance?

BIBLIOGRAPHY

Ackley, Kristina, and Crisina Stanciu, eds. *Laura Cornelius Kellogg: Our Democracy and the American Indian and Other Works.* New York: Syracuse University Press, 2015.

Adams, David Wallace. *Education for Extinction: American Indians and the Boarding School Experience, 1875–1928.* 3rd ed. Lawrence: University Press of Kansas, 1995.

Anderson, Fred. *Crucible of War: The Seven Years' War and the Fate of Empire in British North America, 1754–1766.* Reprint ed. New York: Vintage, 2001.

Anderson, Gary C. *Kinsmen of Another Kind: Dakota White Relations in Upper Mississippi Valley 1650–1862.* St. Paul: Minnesota Historical Society Press, 1997.

Andersson, Rani-Henrik. *The Lakota Ghost Dance of 1890.* Lincoln: University of Nebraska Press, 2008.

Ball, Eve. *Indeh.* Provo, UT: Brigham Young University Press,1982.

Bernstein, Allison R. *American Indians and World War II: Toward a New Era in Indian Affairs.* Norman: University of Oklahoma Press, 1991.

Biolsi, Thomas. *Organizing the Lakota: The Political Economy of the New Deal on the Pine Ridge and Rosebud Reservations.* Reprint ed. Tucson: University of Arizona Press, 1998.

Blee, Lisa. *Framing Chief Leschi: Narratives and the Politics of Historical Justice.* Chapel Hill: The University of North Carolina Press, 2014.

Bowes, John P. *Land Too Good for Indians: Northern Indian Removal.* Norman: University of Oklahoma Press, 2016.

Britten, Thomas. *American Indians in World War I: At Home and at War.* Albuquerque: University of New Mexico Press, 1999.

Bruyneel, Kevin. *The Third Space of Sovereignty: The Postcolonial Politics of U.S.–Indigenous Relations.* Minneapolis: University of Minnesota Press, 2007.

Calloway, Colin G. *New Worlds for All: Indians, Europeans, and the Remaking of Early America.* Baltimore: Johns Hopkins University Press, 1997.

———. *The American Revolution in Indian Country: Crisis and Diversity in Native American Communities.* Cambridge, UK: Cambridge University Press, 1995.

———. *The Scratch of a Pen: 1763 and the Transformation of North America.* New York: Oxford University Press, 2006.

Calloway, Colin G., ed. *Our Hearts Fell to the Ground: Plains Indian Views of How the West Was Lost.* Reprint ed. Boston/New York: Bedford/St. Martin's, 1996.

Castile, George Pierre. *To Show Heart: Native American Self-Determination and Federal Indian Policy, 1960–1975.* Tucson: University of Arizona Press, 1998.

Cattelino, Jessica R. *High Stakes: Florida Seminole Gaming and Sovereignty.* Durham, NC: Duke University Press, 2008.

Child, Brenda J. *Boarding School Seasons: American Indian Families, 1900–1940.* Lincoln: University of Nebraska Press, 2000.

Clark, Blue. Lone Wolf v. Hitchcock*: Treaty Rights and Indian Law at the End of the Nineteenth Century.* Lincoln: University of Nebraska Press, 1994.

Cobb, Daniel M. *Native Activism in Cold War America: The Struggle for Sovereignty*. Lawrence: University Press of Kansas, 2008.

Cothran, Boyd. *Remembering the Modoc War: Redemptive Violence and the Making of American Innocence*. Chapel Hill: The University of North Carolina Press, 2014.

Cowger, Thomas W. *The National Congress of American Indians: The Founding Years*. Lincoln: University of Nebraska Press, 1999.

Crosby, Alfred W. *The Columbian Exchange: Biological and Cultural Consequences of 1492*. Westport, CT: Greenwood Press, 1972.

Davis, Julie L. *Survival Schools: The American Indian Movement and Community Education in the Twin Cities*. Minneapolis: University of Minnesota Press, 2013.

Deloria, Philip. *Indians in Unexpected Places*. Lawrence: University Press of Kansas, 2004.

Deloria, Vine, Jr. *Custer Died for Your Sins: An Indian Manifesto*. New York: Macmillan Company, 1969.

———. *Red Earth, White Lies: Native Americans and the Myth of Scientific Fact*. New York: Scribner, 1995.

Deloria, Vine, Jr., and Clifford Lytle. *The Nations Within: The Past and Future of American Indian Sovereignty*. New York: Pantheon Books, 1984.

DeMallie, Raymond J. "'These Have No Ears': Narrative and Ethnohistorical Method." *Ethnohistory* 40, no. 4 (1993): 515–538.

———. "The Lakota Ghost Dance: An Ethnohistorical Account." *Pacific Historical Review* 51 (Nov. 1982): 385–405.

Denetdale, Jennifer Nez. *Reclaiming Diné History: The Legacies of Navajo Chief Manuelito and Juanita.* Tucson: University of Arizona Press, 2007.

Dowd, Gregory Evans. *A Spirited Resistance: The North American Indian Struggle for Unity, 1745–1815.* Baltimore: Johns Hopkins University Press, 1993.

———. *War Under Heaven: Pontiac, the Indian Nations, and the British Empire.* Baltimore: Johns Hopkins University Press, 2004.

DuVal, Kathleen. *Independence Lost: Lives on the Edge of the American Revolution.* New York: Random House, 2015.

———. *The Native Ground: Indians and Colonists in the Heart of the Continent.* Philadelphia: University of Pennsylvania Press, 2007.

Edmunds, R. David. *The Shawnee Prophet.* Reprint ed. Lincoln: University of Nebraska Press, 1985.

Ellis, Clyde. *A Dancing People: Powwow Culture on the Southern Plains.* Lawrence: University Press of Kansas, 2003.

Erdoes, Richard, and Alfonso Ortiz, eds. *American Indian Myths and Legends.* New York: Pantheon Books, 1984.

Ethridge, Robbie, and Sheri M. Shuck-Hall, eds. *Mapping the Mississippian Shatter Zone: The Colonial Indian Slave Trade and Regional Instability in the American South.* Lincoln: University of Nebraska Press, 2009.

Fenn, Elizabeth A. *Encounters at the Heart of the World: A History of the Mandan People.* Reprint ed. New York: Hill and Wang, 2015.

Fenton, William N. *The Great Law and the Longhouse: A Political History of the Iroquois Confederacy.* Norman: University of Oklahoma Press, 2010.

Fixico, Donald Lee. *Termination and Relocation: Federal Indian Policy, 1945–1960*. Albuquerque: University of New Mexico Press, 1986.

Green, Michael D. *The Politics of Creek Removal: Creek Government and Society in Crisis*. Lincoln: University of Nebraska Press, 1985.

Hämäläinen, Pekka. *The Comanche Empire*. New Haven, CT: Yale University Press, 2009.

Harring, Sidney L. *Crow Dog's Case: American Indian Sovereignty, Tribal Law, and United States Law in the Nineteenth Century*. Cambridge, UK: Cambridge University Press, 1994.

Harvard Project on American Indian Economic Development. *The State of the Native Nations: Conditions under U.S. Policies of Self-Determination*. New York: Oxford University Press, 2007.

Hauptman, Laurence M. *Between Two Fires: American Indians in the Civil War*. New York: Free Press, 1995.

Hoxie, Frederick E. *A Final Promise: The Campaign to Assimilate the Indians, 1880–1920*. Lincoln: University of Nebraska Press, 2001.

Hoxie, Frederick E., and Jay T. Nelson, eds. *Lewis & Clark and the Indian Country: The Native American Perspective*. Champaign: University of Illinois Press, 2007.

Hoxie, Frederick E., ed. *Talking Back to Civilization: Indian Voices from the Progressive Era*. Boston/New York: Bedford/St. Martin's, 2001.

Hudson, Charles M. *Conversations with the High Priest of Coosa*. Chapel Hill: The University of North Carolina Press, 2003.

———. *Knights of Spain, Warriors of the Sun: Hernando De Soto and the South's Ancient Chiefdoms*. Athens: University of Georgia Press, 1997.

Hurtado, Albert L. *Indian Survival on the California Frontier*. Rev. ed. New Haven, CT: Yale University Press, 1990.

Isenberg, Andrew C. *The Destruction of the Bison: An Environmental History, 1750–1920*. Cambridge, UK: Cambridge University Press, 2001.

Iverson, Peter. *Diné: A History of the Navajos*. Albuquerque: University of New Mexico Press, 2002.

Jacoby, Karl. *Shadows at Dawn: An Apache Massacre and the Violence of History*. Reprint ed. London: Penguin Books, 2009.

Jennings, Francis. *Empire of Fortune: Crowns, Colonies, and Tribes in the Seven Years War in America*. Revised ed. New York: W. W. Norton & Company, 1990.

Johnson, Troy R., Joane Nagel, and Duane Champagne, eds. *American Indian Activism: Alcatraz to the Longest Walk*. Champaign: University of Illinois Press, 1997.

Kelman, Ari. *A Misplaced Massacre: Struggling over the Memory of Sand Creek*. Reprint ed. Cambridge, MA: Harvard University Press, 2015.

Klein, Kerwin Lee. *Frontiers of Historical Imagination: Narrating the European Conquest of Native America, 1890–1990*. Reprint ed. Berkeley: University of California Press, 1999.

Knaut, Andrew L. *The Pueblo Revolt of 1680: Conquest and Resistance in Seventeenth-Century New Mexico*. Revised ed. Norman: University of Oklahoma Press, 1995.

Kohlhoff, Dean. *When the Wind Was a River: Aleut Evacuation in World War II*. Seattle: University of Washington Press in association with Aleutian/Pribilof Islands Association, Anchorage, 1995.

Krouse, Susan Applegate. *North American Indians in the Great War.* Lincoln: University of Nebraska Press, 2009.

Lepore, Jill. *The Name of War: King Philip's War and the Origins of American Identity.* New York: Knopf, 1998.

Lookingbill, Brad D. *War Dance at Fort Marion: Plains Indian War Prisoners.* Norman: University of Oklahoma Press, 2014.

Mandell, Daniel R. *King Phillip's War.* New York: Chelsea, 2008.

Mann, Charles C. *1491: New Revelations of the Americas before Columbus.* New York: Knopf, 2006.

———. *1493: Uncovering the New World Columbus Created.* New York: Knopf, 2011.

Marshall, Joseph M., III. *The Journey of Crazy Horse: A Lakota History.* Reprint ed. London: Penguin Books, 2005.

Martin, Joel W. *Sacred Revolt: The Muskogees' Struggle for a New World.* Boston: Beacon Press, 1991.

Mathes, Valerie Sherer, and Richard Lowitt. *The Standing Bear Controversy: Prelude to Indian Reform.* Champaign: University of Illinois Press, 2003.

Maynor Lowery, Malinda. *Lumbee Indians in the Jim Crow South: Race, Identity, and the Making of a Nation.* Chapel Hill: The University of North Carolina Press, 2010.

McMillen, Christian W. *Making Indian Law: The Hualapai Land Case and the Birth of Ethnohistory.* New Haven, CT: Yale University Press, 2007.

Meltzer, David J. *First Peoples in a New World: Colonizing Ice Age America.* Berkeley: University of California Press, 2009.

Merrell, James H. *Into the American Woods: Negotiations on the Pennsylvania Frontier.* New York: W. W. Norton & Company, 2000.

———. *The Indians' New World: Catawbas and Their Neighbors from European Contact through the Era of Removal.* 2nd ed. Chapel Hill: The University of North Carolina Press, 2010.

Miles, Tiya. *Ties That Bind: The Story of an Afro-Cherokee Family in Slavery and Freedom.* 2nd ed. Berkeley: University of California Press, 2015.

Miller, Mark Edwin. *Forgotten Tribes: Unrecognized Indians and the Federal Acknowledgment Process.* Lincoln: University of Nebraska Press, 2004.

Nabokov, Peter. *Where the Lightning Strikes: The Lives of American Indian Sacred Places.* New York: Viking, 2006.

Neihardt, John G. *Black Elk Speaks: Being the Life Story of a Holy Man of the Oglala Sioux.* Lincoln: University of Nebraska Press, 1932.

Nez, Chester, and Judith Schiess Avila. *Code Talker: The First and Only Memoir by One of the Original Navajo Code Talkers of WWII.* New York: Berkley Caliber, 2001.

Norgren, Jill. *The Cherokee Cases: Two Landmark Federal Decisions in the Fight for Sovereignty.* Norman: University of Oklahoma Press, 2004.

Ostler, Jeffrey. *The Plains Sioux and U.S. Colonialism from Lewis and Clark to Wounded Knee.* Cambridge, UK: Cambridge University Pres, 2004.

Parmenter, Jon. *The Edge of the Woods: Iroquoia, 1534–1701.* Lansing: Michigan State University Press, 2014.

Perdue, Theda, and Michael D. Green. *The Cherokee Nation and the Trial of Tears.* Reprint ed. London: Penguin Books, 2008.

Raibmon, Paige. *Authentic Indians: Episodes of Encounter from the Late-Nineteenth-Century Northwest Coast.* Durham, NC: Duke University Press, 2006.

Richter, Daniel K. *Before the Revolution: America's Ancient Pasts.* Cambridge, MA: Belknap Press of Harvard University Press, 2011.

———. *Facing East from Indian Country: A Native History of Early America.* Cambridge, MA: Harvard University Press, 2001.

———. *The Ordeal of the Longhouse: The Peoples of the Iroquois League in the Era of European Colonization.* Chapel Hill: The University of North Carolina Press, 1992.

Rosier, Paul C. *Serving Their Country: American Indian Politics and Patriotism in the Twentieth Century.* Cambridge, MA: Harvard University Press, 2009.

Rountree, Helen C. *The Powhatan Indians of Virginia: Their Traditional Culture.* Norman: University of Oklahoma Press, 1989.

Salish-Pend d'Oreille Culture Committee, Elders Cultural Advisory Council, and Confederated Salish and Kootenai Tribes. *The Salish People.* Lincoln, NE: Bison Books, 2008.

Sando, Joe. *Pueblo Nations: Eight Centuries of Pueblo Indian History.* 2nd printing ed. Santa Fe, NM: Clear Light Books, 1992.

Saunt, Claudio. *West of the Revolution: An Uncommon History of 1776.* New York: W. W. Norton & Company, 2015.

Shreve, Bradley Glenn. *Red Power Rising: The National Indian Youth Council and the Origins of Native Activism.* Norman: University of Oklahoma Press, 2001.

Silva, Noenoe K. *Aloha Betrayed: Native Hawaiian Resistance to American Colonialism.* Durham, NC: Duke University Press, 2004.

Sims, Lowery Stokes. *Fritz Scholder: Indian/Not Indian*. Munich, Germany: Prestel, 2011.

Sioui, Georges E. *Huron Wendat: The Heritage of the Circle*. Rev. ed. Lansing: Michigan State University Press, 2000.

Sleeper-Smith, Susan. *Indian Women and French Men: Rethinking Cultural Encounter in the Western Great Lakes*. Amherst: University of Massachusetts Press, 2001.

Sleeper-Smith, Susan, Juliana Barr, Jean M. O'Brien, Nancy Shoemaker, and Scott Manning Stevens, eds. *Why You Can't Teach United States History without American Indians*. Chapel Hill: The University of North Carolina Press, 2015.

Smith, Paul Chaat. *Everything You Know about Indians Is Wrong*. Minneapolis: University of Minnesota Press, 2009.

Smith, Paul Chaat, and Robert Allen Warrior. *Like a Hurricane: The Indian Movement from Alcatraz to Wounded Knee*. New York: New Press, 1996.

Smoak, Gregory Ellis. *Ghost Dances and Identity: Prophetic Religion and American Indian Ethnogenesis in the Nineteenth Century*. Berkeley: University of California Press, 2006.

Standing Bear, Luther. *My People the Sioux*. 2nd ed. Lincoln, NE: Bison Books, 2006.

Stewart, Omer Call. *Peyote Religion: A History*. Norman: University of Oklahoma Press, 1987.

Tanner, Helen Hornbeck. "The Glaize of 1792: A Composite Indian Community." *Ethnohistory* 25 (1978): 15–39.

Thomas, David Hurst. *Skull Wars: Kennewick Man, Archaeology, and the Battle for Native American Identity*. New York: Basic Books, 2000.

Townsend, Camilla. *Pocahontas and the Powhatan Dilemma*. New York: Hill and Wang, 2004.

Trigger, Bruce G. *The Children of Aataentsic: A History of the Huron People to 1660*. Montreal, Quebec/Kingston, Ontario, CA: McGill-Queen's University Press, 1987.

Troutman, John William. *Indian Blues: American Indians and the Politics of Music, 1879–1934*. Norman: University of Oklahoma Press, 2009.

Vizenor, Gerald Robert. *Manifest Manners: Postindian Warriors of Survivance*. Middletown, CT: Wesleyan University Press, 1994.

Wenger, Tisa Joy. *We Have a Religion: The 1920s Pueblo Indian Dance Controversy and American Religious Freedom*. Chapel Hill: Published in association with the William P. Clements Center for Southwest Studies, Southern Methodist University, by The University of North Carolina Press: 2009.

West, Elliott. *The Last Indian War: The Nez Perce Story*. New York: Oxford University Press, 2011.

White, Richard. *The Middle Ground: Indians, Empires, and Republics in the Great Lakes Region, 1650–1815*. Cambridge, UK: Cambridge University Press, 1991.

Wilkins, David E. *American Indian Sovereignty and the U.S. Supreme Court: The Masking of Justice*. University of Texas PR ed. Austin: University of Texas Press, 1997.

Wilkins, David E., and K. Tsianina Lomawaima. *Uneven Ground: American Indian Sovereignty and Federal Law*. Norman: University of Oklahoma Press, 2002.

Wilkinson, Charles F. *Blood Struggle: The Rise of Modern Indian Nations*. New York: Norton, 2005.

Williams, Robert A., Jr. *Like a Loaded Weapon: The Rehnquist Court, Indian Rights, and the Legal History of Racism in America*. Minneapolis: University of Minnesota Press, 2005.

———. *Linking Arms Together: American Indian Treaty Visions of Law and Peace, 1600–1800*. Revised ed. Abingdon, UK: Routledge, 1999.

IMAGE CREDITS

Page 7: © Shchipkova Elena/Shutterstock.
Page 15: © SumikoPhoto/iStock/Thinkstock.
Page 17: © Georgios Kollidas/iStock/Thinkstock.
Page 21: © Library of Congress, Prints and Photographs Division, LC-USZ62-354
Page 25: © Phil_Henke/iStock/Thinkstock.
Page 30: © Oleksiy Khmyz/iStock/Thinkstock.
Page 35: © Richard Gunion/iStock/Thinkstock.
Page 39: © SF photo/Shutterstock.
Page 47: © Library of Congress, Washington/Wikimedia Commons/Public Domain.
Page 57: © Wikimedia Commons/Public Domain.
Page 62: © Tempusfugit/iStock/Thinkstock.
Page 71: © Christopher Paquette/iStock/Thinkstock.
Page 78: © GeorgiosArt/iStock/Thinkstock.
Page 83: © Adam Parent/Shutterstock.
Page 87: © Vera Anima/Shutterstock.
Page 94: © The Clay Machine Gun/Shutterstock.
Page 99: © Stocksnapper/Shutterstock.
Page 102: © QueGar3/iStock/Thinkstock.
Page 107: © MichelleLyles/iStock/Thinkstock.
Page 110: © fdastudillo/iStock/Thinkstock.
Page 115: © jesiotr9/iStock/Thinkstock.
Page 119: © DennyThurstonPhotography/iStock/Thinkstock.

Page 123: © Library of Congress, Prints and Photographs Division, LC-USZ62-131515

Page 127: © Marzolino/Shutterstock.

Page 133: © Library of Congress, Prints and Photographs Division, LC-USZ62-12277

Page 134: © Dja65/Shutterstock.

Page 140: © TiSanti/iStock/Thinkstock.

Page 143: © Library of Congress, Prints and Photographs Division, LC-USZ62-56421.

Page 148: © digitalfarmer/iStock/Thinkstock.

Page 156: © steve estvanik/Shutterstock.

Page 159: © Library of Congress, Prints and Photographs Division, LC-USF33-T01-001569-M4.

Page 167: © Wikimedia Commons/CC-BY-SA-3.0.

Page 170: © Kris_art/iStock/Thinkstock.

Page 175: © Library of Congress, Prints and Photographs Division, LC-DIG-ppmsca-04302.

Page 178: © Maciej Bledowski/iStock/Thinkstock.

Page 182: © Eric Krouse/Shutterstock.

Page 187: © Silver Spiral Arts/Shutterstock.

Page 190: © Lik Studio/Shutterstock.

NOTES

NOTES